Like most Australians, DAVID DALE learned very little about Australia at school. He graduated from Sydney University with honours in psychology, but got his education working as a political reporter for *The Australian*, features editor of *The Sun–Herald*, editor of *The Bulletin*, breakfast announcer for ABC radio and New York correspondent for *The Sydney Morning Herald*. He is currently anthropology and media writer for *The Sydney Morning Herald*, and contributes regularly on travel and popular culture to *The Age* and the ABC. His nine books include *Essential Places, An Australian in America, The 100 Things Everyone Needs to know About Italy,* and *The Obsessive Traveller, or Why I Don't Steal Towels From Great Hotels Any More.*

CATHY WILCOX was born in Sydney in 1963 and grew up with an eye for the blank spaces between blocks of text on a page. She has decorated spaces in at least fourteen children's books, including *A Proper Little Lady* and *Boris and Bowch*, and provided the blocks of text as well in *Enzo The Wonderfish*. Cathy now takes filling in the blanks to its logical conclusion by drawing cartoons for *The Sydney Morning Herald* (since 1989) and *The Age* (since 1993) and has published a collection of cartoons called *Throw Away Lines*.

THE 100

THINGS EVERYONE NEEDS TO KNOW
ABOUT
AUSTRALIA

DAVID DALE

Illustrations by Cathy Wilcox

PAN
Pan Macmillan Australia

First published 1996 in Pan by Pan Macmillan Australia Pty Limited
St Martins Tower, 31 Market Street, Sydney

This edition revised and updated 1999
Reprinted (revised and updated) 1996, 1997, 1999

National Library of Australia Cataloguing-in-Publication data:

Dale, David, 1948–.
    The 100 things everyone needs to know about Australia.

    (Rev. ed.).
    ISBN 0 330 36171 6.

    1. Australia. I. Title. II. Title: One hundred things everyone needs to
    know about Australia.

994

Typeset in 10.2/13pt Sabon by Midland Typesetters Pty Ltd, Maryborough,
Victoria
Printed in Australia by McPherson's Printing Group

contents

CONTENTS

introduction

If Australia's education system was perfect, and if every Australian had a perfect memory, this book wouldn't be necessary. But it isn't and we don't, so this is the next best thing.

In theory, this book contains the minimum information that every Australian needs in order to function in modern society—the vital stuff we forgot from our schooling and all the useful stuff they never taught us. In theory, this book is the only reference work that should be in every Australian home, and the first guide for any visitor who wants to understand our culture. In theory, I should be a millionaire by this time next year.

In practice, of course, you could set 100 authors the task of listing the essential knowledge for Australians and they'd produce 100 different books. What one person considers crucial data is someone else's trivia quiz. But somebody had to start the ball rolling, and I was the fool who nominated himself.

My plan was that this would be a very small book—just 100 crisp paragraphs, each summarising some helpful fact or idea. Each bold assertion was meant simply to point the way to further reading for those who had the time, while giving busy readers enough to bluff their way through everyday conversations ... Patrick White's most accessible book is *Voss*, Australia was discovered 50 000 years ago by Indonesians, Vegemite is American-owned, Grange Hermitage is our greatest red wine (but Jasper Hill shiraz is better value), Gough Whitlam was our most interesting politician. And so on. A bit of history, a bit of culture, a bit of sociology, some practical advice, and home for tea.

Then I made the mistake of getting too interested in what I was researching, and of wanting to tell people about it, and the result is that this book should really be called 'The 3000 Things Everyone Needs To Know About Australia'. Just look at the index.

I must admit that I included some things because I thought they were interesting, even when I suspected they were not essential. I mean, you could probably get through life without knowing that this continent might have been called Psitaccoria instead of Australia (see chapter 5) or that the world's first call girl service was operating in Melbourne in 1891 (see chapter 99). I also couldn't resist throwing in a couple of provocative ideas as talking points—such as the case for abolition of state governments and the need to add an octopus to the coat of arms.

Now that the manuscript is with the publisher, the worries have started. I just know that the day this book appears, I'm going to think of 100 more vital facts I forgot to include. I wonder if there should be a chapter that gives the phone number for emergencies (000), the speed limit in built-up areas (60 kph) and how much alcohol you can drink and still be allowed to drive if stopped by a police breathalyser (two glasses of wine in an hour). But where would I stop?

The best judge of what is missing is you. If you notice any glaring omissions—any fact that you think every Australian needs to know but which I have failed to include—or if you find any errors, please write to me care of the publishers. I hope to do regular updates and, between us, we can make this book perfect by the year 2000.

The following publications have been valuable sources of information and inspiration during my researches, and I commend them to those who want to go deeper into this country's essential knowledge: *Year Book Australia 1997* (published by the Australian Bureau of Statistics); *Book of Australian Facts* (Reader's Digest); *Reinventing Australia* by Hugh Mackay (HarperCollins); *The Australian Book of Lists* by Michael Morton Evans (Simon and Schuster); *Suburban Icons* by Steve Bedwell (ABC Books); *Australian Icons* by Peter Luck (William Heinemann); *The New Guinness Book of Records 1997* (Guinness Publishing); *Great Australian Sporting Heroes* (The Five Mile Press); *The Fatal Shore* by Robert Hughes (Collins Harvill); *The Dictionary of Famous Australians* by Ann Atkinson (Allen and Unwin); *Chronicle of the 20th Century* (Chronicle Penguin); *The Book of Australian Firsts* (Guinness);

The New Shell Book of Firsts by Patrick Robertson (Headline); *One Continuous Picnic—A History of Australian Eating*, by Michael Symons (Duck Press); *What Happened When* by Anthony Barker (Allen and Unwin).

My profound thanks to Cathy Wilcox for her incisive cartoons, Nikki Christer, Julia Taylor and Sandra Horth at Pan Macmillan for making the project happen, and to Susan Williams and Amelia Dale for tolerating six months of mental distraction and the ever-growing mounds of paper and books all over the loungeroom.

The pace of social change in Australia is so fast that this book needs to be substantially rewritten every 18 months or so. When I was first putting it together at the beginning of 1996, Paul Keating was the prime minister, we were heading towards a republic, and we knew nothing of Pauline Hanson, *Titanic*, Cate Blanchett, Olympic scandals, Michael Hutchence's belt, and Mark Taylor's retirement from Test cricket. Many readers suggested improvements to the first and second editions, and thanks to them, this 2000 edition is a more thorough summary of a nation's collective wisdom. I'd welcome more letters about this edition, so that the first edition of the next millennium can achieve perfection.

DAVID DALE
JUNE 1999

1

where we live

*f*orget the image of bush battlers pioneering through the sweeping plains of a wide brown land. Australia is the most urbanised nation on earth. Nearly 80 per cent of the 18.5 million people on this continent live in just ten cities, all of them beside the sea. It's as if we're clinging desperately to the coastline waiting for somebody to sail back and take us home. So instead of a bronzed farmer in a broad-brimmed hat, our national stereotype should be a suited office worker, or a surfer in board shorts.

Most of this country is empty. We have the lowest population density in the world: 2 people per square kilometre, compared with 3 per square kilometre in Canada, 26 in the United States, 99 in Indonesia, 238 in Britain and 327 in Japan.

In fact, the word 'urbanised' is not quite an accurate description of Australians. A better word would be suburbanised. About 70 per cent of Australians are currently paying off houses in the suburbs. We have one of the highest levels of home ownership in the world. The most popular dwelling unit is the detached brick house with red tiled roof, front lawn and back garden (fitted with Hills Hoist and barbecue, of course). As a federal government report early in 1995 noted:

> Undoubtedly suburbia is a hallmark of Australian urban life and it is aspired to by both the Australian born and immigrants. Suburban growth offers considerable positive attributes for individuals and society. It offers space. It provides housing that is affordable and of very high quality for a large range of household types and socioeconomic classes.

But the report noted governments had failed to meet their obligations in providing services for suburbanites. They still have to come into town for a decent cup of coffee.

2

the newer arrivals

*b*etween the 1950s and the 1990s, Australia transformed itself from one of the dullest nations on earth to one of the most interesting. The principal reason for this was the arrival of five million immigrants from Europe and Asia, part of a policy of population-boosting introduced soon after World War Two. Slowly and sometimes painfully, the newcomers introduced their skills and ideas into a conservative culture, and persuaded the earlier settlers of the virtues of diversity.

The census of 1947 showed that 90 per cent of the population was born in Australia, with a further 8 per cent born in Britain or New Zealand. At that time, any foreigner wishing to live here came up against the White Australia Policy. The Immigration Restriction Act of 1901 specified that intending immigrants had to pass a dictation test 'in a European language'. It was amazing how many Africans and Asians did not understand a word of Gaelic or Romanian. The policy was officially changed in 1959 but

3

operated informally until 1973, when the Whitlam Labor Government passed a law which specified 'the avoidance of discrimination on any grounds of race or colour of skin'.

Today, 78 per cent of the population was born in Australia, with 6 per cent born in Britain, 2 per cent in New Zealand, 2 per cent in Italy, 1.5 per cent in the former Yugoslavia, 1.5 per cent in China or Hong Kong, 1 per cent Greece and 1 per cent Vietnam. Some 3.9 million Australians were born overseas and a further 3.6 million had one or both parents born overseas. About 16 per cent of the population speaks a language other than English at home.

Immigration has been reduced dramatically in recent years, so that now Australia receives only 70 000 new citizens a year. The latest arrivals tend to be smarter than we are—11.4 per cent are 'managers and administrators' (compared with 10.9 per cent of Old Aussies) and 34 per cent are 'professionals' (compared with 13.7 per cent of OAs). The major points of origin are still Britain and Ireland (13 per cent), New Zealand (13 per cent), China including Hong Kong (12 per cent) Vietnam (5 per cent), and the Philippines (4 per cent). The claim by local conservatives that Australia is being 'Asianised' is not sustained by the statistics, more's the pity.

3
the Coat of Arms

Y ou can eat the Australian Coat of Arms, using the shield in the middle as a plate, although the kangaroo will taste a lot better than the emu. And you need not worry that you may be endangering native animals. Emus, the second largest bird in the world (after the ostrich), are now farmed for their meat (and oil and skin and feathers). And it has recently been established that there are about 40 million kangaroos in Australia.

The emu's meat is pretty tough, and is best served minced up (in ravioli, for example) or salted and thinly sliced, like prosciutto. The kangaroo's meat is lean, and high in iron and protein. It is best served seared on the outside and rare in the middle, accompanied by a beetroot puree.

Kangaroos were commonly eaten by Aborigines before the Europeans arrived but, during most of the 20th century, their consumption by humans was banned by state governments for misplaced health reasons. Following changes to state laws in the early 1990s, human consumption of kangaroo meat is now legal in most of Australia, though many restaurants are not yet confident in preparing it.

The Coat of Arms was originally granted to

Australia in 1908, but that version featured a shield containing a cross decorated with five stars. The state governments got stroppy that they weren't represented, so in 1912 a new version was approved by King George V, in which the shield contained the badges of the six states.

It's about time the Coat of Arms was updated to reflect modern reality. My suggestion is to add an octopus in the middle, seated on the shield, with arms round the emu and arms round the roo. The octopus (another native animal) would symbolise the way we've changed from a boring nation to an interesting nation in a single generation.

Back in the 1950s, Australians of English origin would not dream of eating octopus. They used it as bait. Now, as the result of the European and Asian immigrants who have become part of our life, octopus—chilli coated and char grilled—is the trendiest dish in Australia's inner-city bistros. Such a sign of our adventurousness, and of the fact that most Australians live by the sea, would give the Coat of Arms a new relevance.

4

size

*a*ustralia is big—but try telling that to the tourists who arrive thinking they can cover the Barrier Reef and the Tasmanian wilderness and Ayers Rock and Perth in a five-day visit. With a surface area of 7.6 million square kilometres, it could swallow all of Europe and still have room for Turkey and Scandinavia. It is almost the same size as the United States, unless the Americans cheat and try to include Alaska (which is really in Canada).

Crossing Australia takes five hours by plane, and three days by train, and there is a two-hour time difference between the east coast and the west coast. Australia has 36 735 kilometres of coastline, which means we have more beaches than any other nation. (Seven thousand of them.) The tallest point is the top of Mount Kosciusko, which is 2228 metres up—pretty pathetic by world mountain standards.

Australia is the lowest, the flattest and the driest continent, with about a

NEXT
5000
KM

quarter of its surface classified as uninhabitable. The largest of our deserts, the Great Sandy in the north of Western Australia, covers 414 000 square kilometres and is as big as England.

Australia is also a long way from everywhere else. The distance from Sydney to London is 17 000 kilometres, a 24-hour flight. The distance from Sydney to Los Angeles is 12 000 kilometres, a 13-hour flight. So Australians take their travel seriously.

5
discoveries

a ustralia was discovered more than 55 000 years ago by people sailing down from the islands we now know as Indonesia and New Guinea. (Just how much more than 55 000 years ago is the subject of debate by scholars, and one group claims to have dated rock engravings at Jinmium, north-western Australia, as more than 100 000 years old.)

Arriving in waves every few thousand years, the original Australian immigrants settled the northern areas and gradually moved south. The earliest confirmed evidence of human habitation has been found in the form of coloured rocks, possibly used as crayons, which are buried in a cave called Malakunaja 2 in Kakadu National Park in the Northern Territory. They are more than 50 000 years old (at the time, it was possible to walk from New Guinea to Tasmania without getting your feet wet). Stone tools found near the Nepean River, west of Sydney, have been dated as 45 000 years old; there are signs of a 40 000-year-old campsite near what is now Melbourne Airport; and remains found in Warreen Cave, west of Hobart, seem to be 35 000 years old.

The bones of an Aboriginal woman who was cremated 35 000 years ago have been found near Lake Mungo in far western New South Wales. It was the world's earliest known cremation. She lived in what may have been Australia's first city—continuously inhabited by people who built ovens to cook the abundance of local fish and animals, until the lakes dried up about 15 000 years ago.

About 500 years ago some other seafarers from much further north started bumping into the shores of Australia. The first officially confirmed landing by Europeans was in March 1606, when a Dutch ship called the *Duyfken* encountered the residents of far north Queensland at the mouth of what is now the Pennefather River. The ship departed rapidly when one of the crewmen was speared to death.

Another Dutchman, Dirck Hartog, landed at what is now Shark Bay, Western Australia in 1616 and named the country Eendrachtsland, after his ship. He staked his claim by nailing a pewter plate to a tree. The plate is now in the Rijksmuseum in Amsterdam. The Dutch did a fair bit of mapping of the western and southern shores of the continent, and were starting to assess the viability of a Dutch colony around the time a ship called the *Endeavour* set off from England under the command of James Cook in 1768.

The *Endeavour* was carrying a load of British scientists to the Pacific Ocean so they could observe the planet Venus crossing the sun. They got a bonus. They were able to map a couple of islands that were later called New Zealand, and they spent 75 days exploring the east coast of the huge island which the Dutch were calling Hollandia Nova (New Holland). After Cook landed at Botany Bay (so called because the botanist Joseph Banks found so many specimens there), he claimed the area for Britain, and called it New South Wales.

Eendrachtsland, New Holland, New South Wales—none of them were great candidates for naming of the great southern continent. There was a better one. One explorer in the early 18th century had noticed the huge variety of colourful and noisy parrots along the coastline, and produced a map which christened the continent Terra Psittacorum— the land of parrots. Should we count it a lucky escape that we're not now living in Psittacoria?

6
what we know

*a*ustralia's education system is under challenge for its irrelevance to the needs of future citizens. A government-appointed committee called the Civics Expert Group, which included a history professor from Melbourne and a director-general of education from Sydney, produced a report in 1995 which said:

> Many young Australians can tell you the scientific names of a pantheon of dinosaurs, and regale you with the names and relative sizes of the planets; they can list the islands of Japan and give you a detailed description of the building of the pyramids. Few, however, can tell you anything about Federation, or name six great Australians in the arts, science or politics.

Now that you have bought this book, you will have no problem with the mysteries raised in the last sentence of that quote* but, at the time the Civics Expert Group was writing, this book did not exist.

---

* Federation was the unification in 1901 of the six English colonies within Australia into a single nation with a central government and six state governments. Six great Australians would be Germaine Greer, Arthur Boyd, Macfarlane Burnet, Howard Florey, Gough Whitlam, Robert Menzies.

The report went on to say:

It is clear that our young people are leaving school without sufficient knowledge and understanding of Australia's political and social heritage, its democratic processes and government, its judicial system and its system of public administration. In the absence of an adequate understanding of how our society works, without the skill and confidence to participate effectively, and lacking attachment to civic values, they simply cannot be effective citizens.

To prove its point, the Expert Group commissioned a survey of what Australians know about their democratic structures. It found:

only 19 per cent of people have some understanding of what Federation meant for Australia's system of government. Only 40 per cent can name the two federal houses of parliament, and only 24 per cent know that senators are elected on a state-wide basis. Only 33 per cent have some knowledge of the rights and responsibilities of citizens.**

The group concluded that education in 'civics' should be compulsory in primary and secondary schools: 'Education for citizenship ranks with

** Federation meant a whole lot of extra politicians and confusion over who had the power to do what. The chambers of federal parliament are the House of Representatives and the Senate. It's compulsory to vote in all elections (or be fined)—but you can write anything you like on your ballot paper.

English and mathematics as a priority for school education.'

The Federal Government took two years to ponder the report, and in mid 1997, allocated $17.4 million to help State Education Departments introduce civics courses in primary and secondary schools. The compulsory curriculum will include 'principles of democracy, government in Australia, and events which shaped the nation's identity'. The government hoped the new courses would be introduced in 1999, but progress has been slow. Meanwhile, those who have already passed through the Australian education system will need to read this book.

7

our stars

*t*he former Prime Minister, Paul Keating, had to warn Australians in 1995 about the danger of moving from 'the cultural cringe to the cultural swagger'. The cultural cringe was the assumption that prevailed till the 1970s that nothing Australians did could be as good as anything done overseas, and top creative people had to be imported from Britain and America. The cultural swagger is an assumption growing in the 1990s that we make the best movies, meals, models, music, soap operas and sports champions, and we have nothing to learn from other countries. It's certainly true that Australians start to assume the strutting posture when we shortlist the entertainers who have found international fame . . .

☆ **JOAN SUTHERLAND,**
a tall Sydney soprano
nicknamed La
Stupenda, whose Lucia
di Lammermoor took
her round the world,
and whose doubts
about Australia's

15

multiculturalism keep her living in Switzerland.

☆ **SILVERCHAIR**, a teenage rock trio who originated in Newcastle and released successful albums in America. The group's leader, Daniel Johns, offended some of his fellow citizens in 1997 by telling *Rolling Stone* magazine that Newcastle was 'the centre of fucking wankers'.

☆ **GEOFFREY RUSH**, a Brisbane-born stage actor who won the Best Actor Oscar in 1997 for playing a mentally disturbed pianist called David Helfgott in the film *Shine*, and was nominated in 1999 for best supporting actor in *Shakespeare In Love*.

☆ **OLIVIA NEWTON-JOHN**, an English-born and Melbourne-educated singer who starred in the US movie *Grease*, was named America's top female country vocalist in 1974, and had a pop hit with 'Let's Get Physical' in 1981. In the mid 1990s she had surgery for breast cancer.

☆ **KYLIE MINOGUE**, a short Melbourne actor who was able to convert her role in the soap opera 'Neighbours' into a singing career, with particular success in Britain.

☆ **ELLE MACPHERSON**, a tall Sydney model nicknamed 'The Body' who featured in swimsuit spreads in US magazines and now plays small film roles (for example, *Batman and Robin*) and promotes products bearing her name, particularly underwear.

☆ **ANTHONY LaPAGLIA**, an Adelaide actor

who was unknown here but is valued in Hollywood for playing Italian-American cops or killers, and who became the star of the TV series 'Murder One'.

☆ **NICOLE KIDMAN**, a Sydney actor who specialises in playing pale redheads. Her marriage to Tom Cruise is not the reason for her success in *To Die For* and *Batman Forever*.

☆ **CLIVE JAMES**, a Sydney writer of humorous social commentary who moved to Britain and became a TV talk show host.

☆ **INXS** (pronounced 'in excess'), a Perth pop band who became, during the 1980s, Australia's hottest sellers since The Seekers, with sales of eight million for their album *Kick*. In 1997 their singer, Michael Hutchence, was found hanged with his belt in a Sydney hotel room—either suicide or a sexual experiment.

☆ **BARRY HUMPHRIES**, a Melbourne-born comedian and social commentator, who is best known as the acerbic 'housewife superstar' Edna Everage and the gross Australian diplomat Sir Les Patterson. His stage and TV shows succeeded in Britain but failed in America.

☆ **PAUL HOGAN**, a popular TV comedian in Sydney during the 1970s who made one of the world's most profitable films in the 1980s—*Crocodile Dundee*. Then he did tourism commercials in America promising to 'throw another shrimp on the barbie' (when an Aussie would say 'prawn') and left his ageing wife Noelene for his costar Linda Kozlowski. His later movies flopped.

☆ **MEL GIBSON**, a New York-born but Sydney-trained actor whose *Mad Max* caught Hollywood's eye and whose *Lethal Weapon*s have made him rich enough to produce and direct films such as *Braveheart*.

☆ **ERROL FLYNN**, a Hobart-born actor who found Hollywood fame as a swashbuckler in *Captain Blood*, *Robin Hood*, and *The Charge of the Light Brigade* and died in 1959 from the effects of drugs, drink and sexual diseases.

☆ **JUDY DAVIS**, a Perth-born, Sydney-trained actor who is now America's pre-eminent player of neurotic women. She was Oscar nominated for *A Passage to India* and *Husbands and Wives*, but robbed both times.

☆ **BRYAN BROWN**, a limited but likeable Sydney actor whose Hollywood hits include *FX*, *Cocktail* and *Gorillas in the Mist*.

☆ **PETER ALLEN**, a singer/pianist/composer born in Tenterfield, NSW, who briefly married Liza Minnelli and got launched into US cabarets. His 'I Still Call Australia Home' is almost an anthem.

☆ **CATE BLANCHETT**, a theatre actress trained at Sydney's National Institute of Dramatic Art, she came to international notice in *Oscar and Lucinda*, and was Oscar-nominated for *Elizabeth*.

8
Australia Day

*a*ll Australians get a public holiday on 26 January each year to commemorate the day in 1788 when a group of soldiers raised the flag of Britain beside Sydney Harbour to inaugurate a new penal colony. The soldiers were under the command of Arthur Phillip, who had brought 11 ships carrying 770 prisoners on a nine-month voyage from Portsmouth.

If Phillip had followed orders, the Australia Day holiday would be on 18 January, which was when Phillip landed in Botany Bay. On the recommendation of Joseph Banks, the chief botanist with James Cook's expedition of 1770, the British government had determined that this would be the best place to dump its surplus prisoners.

Phillip was shocked to discover that Botany Bay was bleak and windswept and surrounded by swamps. But a little exploration revealed that about 15 kilometres to the north was 'the finest natural harbour in the world, in which a thousand sail of the line may ride

with the most perfect security'. So he started his new settlement in what he called Port Jackson. Between Phillip's first fleet and the arrival of the last convict ship in January 1868 (in Fremantle, Western Australia), a total of 159 000 British prisoners were deposited in Australia. So it's reasonable to say that the majority of Anglo-Australians are descended from criminals.

Phillip never used the term 'Australia Day' for 26 January because, during his four-year term as governor of the colony, the place was known only as New South Wales. The new name was promoted by the explorer Matthew Flinders, based on the Latin term 'Terra Australis' (south land) which, he said, would offend no-one by having 'no reference to the two claiming nations' (Britain and Holland). It was not officially recognised till 1817, when Governor Lachlan Macquarie wrote in a dispatch to London that he was commissioning further explorations of 'the Coasts of the Continent of Australia, which I hope will be the Name given to this Country in future'.

9
the freedom fighter

a ustralia's version of William Tell or Ho Chi Minh or Robin Hood is an Aboriginal leader named Pemulwuy. Between 1790 and 1802, he united the tribes of the Sydney region (the Eora, Dharuk and Tharawal) in a guerilla campaign against the invading forces of Governors Phillip, Hunter and King. He took so many bullets in battles with the British troops that legends grew about his immortality.

The administration offered a reward for his capture which included '20 gallons of spirit, two suits of clothes for a free man, and for anyone already on conditional emancipation, free pardon and recommendation for a passage to England'. It has been argued that if the Colonial Office in Britain had been kept fully informed of how Pemulwuy was demoralising the fragile settlement, they might have decided to give up the whole thing and bring all the white people home.

British troops finally captured Pemulwuy in 1802. His head was slashed off with a sabre, preserved in alcohol and sent to London as a specimen of local fauna. In an accompanying letter, Governor King wrote: 'Altho' a terrible pest to the colony, he was a brave and independent character . . . ' The head's current location is unknown, but it would be a nice gesture for the British government to do a bit of investigating and return it to us.

Tell, Hood and Ho have a multitude of plaques and statues all over their countries. Pemulwuy's name is attached to just one small park in Redfern, Sydney. The site of his biggest battle with the NSW Corps, at the eastern end of George Street, Parramatta, near the river, would be an appropriate place for a plaque, but there is nothing. The difference, of course, is that he lost.

His son Tedbury continued the guerilla war for another eight years after Pemulwuy's death, until the alliance of Sydney tribes fell apart. In a book called *Pemulwuy: The Rainbow Warrior*, Eric Willmot writes:

> The British not only sought to destroy him physically, they, and some of their descendants, attempted to obliterate the very evidence of his existence. Until recently, Pemulwuy's name has never appeared in any white Australian history, yet he lives on in the unpublished records of his enemies, and in the minds of Aboriginal Australians.

10
Anzac Day

*a*ustralians get a national holiday on 25 April, to commemorate one of our biggest military losses. A total of 7600 Australian troops and 2500 New Zealand troops were killed at Gallipoli on the southern coastline of Turkey trying to carry out a British plan to seize the city of Istanbul and force Turkey out of World War One.

Soldiers of the Australian and New Zealand Army Corps landed at Gaba Tepe on the Gallipoli Peninsula on 25 April 1915 and found the hills behind the beach far harder to climb and far better defended than they had been told. A withdrawal was proposed the next day, but they were ordered to dig in and, after eight months of futile attacks on the Turks, they were finally evacuated in December.

It is sometimes argued that the British deliberately sacrificed Australian lives as part of a scheme to distract the Turks. In fact, the British lost 40 000 of their own troops at Gallipoli, so it would appear that the

23

British officers were merely stupid rather than evil.

Nowadays Anzac Day honours Australian soldiers who died in all wars, and veterans of the army, navy and airforce march through the streets of Australia's capital cities in the morning, and share drinks and memories with old comrades in the afternoon. It has tended to replace 26 January as a patriotic symbol because Australia Day has connotations of imperialism, while Anzac Day means simple heroism. As well, 25 April is the one day of the year when the coin-tossing game of two-up is legal in Australian streets, since it was a traditional form of gambling for Australian soldiers. Sadly, not too many people remember how to play it.

11
our language

g rudgingly, Australians have to admit that 'g'day' is not a Hollywood stereotype. We really do greet each other that way. And men really do use the word 'mate'—when they can't remember a name, or they want an alternative to 'um', or they're about to stab someone in the back. The traditional Australian concept of 'mateship' (loyalty to fellow drinkers) and the requirement that men do favours for each other 'under the Old Mates Act' have become tainted in recent times by being used to rationalise corruption in politics and the police force.

Usages that now seem unique to Australian English most often came from obscure dialects spoken by the convicts—like swag (knapsack), larrikin (an amusingly mischievous person), open slather (complete freedom), shout (buy a round of drinks) and skerrick (tiny particle). The original Australians gave us thousands of place names, and contributed about 400 words to everyday modern

Spot the Errors

Strewth, Blue, I'll be frigged if we're gonna get these jumbucks droved by tuckertime

She'll be apples cobbler

Wilcox

conversation—from kangaroo and dingo to 'gone bung' (broken), 'hard yakka' (work) and 'within cooee' (shouting distance).

But many traditional usages are being replaced by Americanisms. Hardly anybody calls women 'sheilas' any more, 'fair dinkum' and 'true blue' would be confined to older denizens of rural areas, and 'cobber' and 'bonzer' went out with the arrival of television in 1956. Bastard and bugger are still affectionate terms of abuse, but 'the great Australian adjective', bloody, has been largely replaced by a more international word starting with F. Sadly, our congratulatory 'goodonya' is giving way to 'go for it'. But we still mystify Americans by referring to an unfashionable person as 'a dag' (literal meaning: a bit of wool from around a sheep's bottom), a pretentious person as a 'wanker' and self-indulgent behaviour as 'a big wank' (the American translation is 'jerk-off').

We'd never throw a shrimp on the barbie (since we call that crustacean a prawn) but we do still like our diminutives. The garbos are likely to have a smoko in the arvo. Unless they're taking a sickie. And no-one would be surprised to receive an invitation to a poolside party in these terms: 'We thought we'd give the kiddies their Chrissie pressies by the barbie this year, so bring some tinnies, your cossie and something to stop the mossies.'

12
poetry

*t*he most famous Australian poem is 'The Man from Snowy River', written in 1890 by Banjo Paterson (whose head is now on the ten dollar note). It is perennially popular, even with school-kids, because of its exciting story and galloping rhythm, and it was made into one of Australia's most successful films. It begins:

> There was movement at the station, for the word
> had passed around
> That the colt from Old Regret had got away,

The second most famous Australian poem is now called 'My Country', although its author originally called it 'Core of My Heart'. She was Dorothea Mackellar, who grew up in the Sydney suburb of Rose Bay in the 1890s and spent much of her life in Britain (where the poem was first published in 1908). It begins:

> The love of field and coppice,
> Of green and shaded lanes,
> Of ordered woods and gardens
> Is running in your veins.

Most Australians only know the second verse, which begins:

> I love a sunburnt country,
> A land of sweeping plains,

But, for Australia's most important popular poem, we have to return to Banjo Paterson. In the same 1895 collection as 'The Man from Snowy River' was a thoughtful discussion which confronted way back then the differences between Australia's rural fantasy and its urban reality. It was 'Clancy of the Overflow', supposedly narrated by someone stuck in a city clerical job and longing to swap with a friend who had 'gone to Queensland droving'. The key lines are:

> And he sees the vision splendid of the sunlit plains extended,
> And at night the wondrous glory of the everlasting stars . . .
> And in place of lowing cattle, I can hear the fiendish rattle
> Of the tramways and the 'buses making hurry down the street;
> And the language uninviting of the gutter children fighting . . .
> For townsfolk have no time to grow, they have no time to waste.

The poem ends with a masterly understatement:

> But I doubt he'd suit the office, Clancy, of The Overflow.

Similar issues are explored by Australia's most famous modern poet, Les Murray, whose *Collected Poems* is a set text in schools and whose *Subhuman Redneck Poems* won the international T. S. Eliot literary prize in 1996. He sees himself as a defender of the disappearing country people and as a baiter of city governments, whom he describes as 'bullies'.

13
the first Australians

*f*rom the arrival of the British, it's been a fast ride downhill for Australia's indigenous population. There were half a million Aboriginal people here in 1788. Now there are 353 000, about 70 per cent of whom live in towns and cities. They fell victim to slaughter by settlers in the course of 'clearing' the land, diseases introduced by the new arrivals, loss of their traditional food and water supplies, and neglect by the authorities. They were not citizens, and had no right to vote. Section 127 of the Australian Constitution, drawn up in 1900, said: 'In reckoning the number of people in the Commonwealth, or of a State or other part of the Commonwealth, aboriginal natives shall not be counted.'

There were two breakthroughs in the 20th century. In a referendum in 1967, white Australians voted overwhelmingly to include Aborigines in the census and give the federal government power to make laws to improve their conditions. Then, in 1982,

We'll make a deal: what's mine is mine, and what's yours is mined

Eddie Mabo and four other people of the Meriam tribe in the Torres Strait Islands asked the High Court to confirm their traditional right to their land. It was a challenge to the legal fiction on which the British had occupied Australia: that the continent was *terra nullius* (no-one's land) because the Aborigines were not capable of ownership.

Arguing the case took ten years, during which Eddie Mabo died, but, in 1992, the High Court ruled in his favour. The decision had huge implications for the land rights of all Aboriginal people. It threw state governments into confusion, and panicked mining companies and farmers. To clarify the situation, the Federal Government passed the *Native Title Act* at the end of 1993. It said, in effect, that Aboriginal Australians who could establish that they had continuously occupied an area since the arrival of the whites would be entitled to own the land or be compensated for infringements on it. A Native Title Tribunal was set up to rule on claims and compensation.

But then in 1996, the High Court, in a ruling called 'the Wik decision', said native title could apply to pastoral leases (land used by private businesses for grazing sheep and cattle, but actually owned by the Government). Pastoral families and companies pressured the government of John Howard into changing the Native Title Act so that Aboriginal rights were reduced and pastoralists were given more control over the land they were leasing.

14
our animals

*a*bout 55 million years ago, the slab of land we now call Australia made its final split from a vast continent called Gondwana, leaving behind Africa, South America, India and Antarctica. The long separation from the rest of the world meant that life here evolved in a unique direction, so we now have the planet's strangest collection of creatures. A few examples . . .

☆ **THE KOALA**, a marsupial (same family as the kangaroo) which lives in gum trees, rears its young in a pouch and has, for its size, the world's longest appendix (to digest the eucalyptus leaves it eats). Koalas have been lucky to survive human habitation this long—hunted first by the Aborigines for food, then by 19th century white settlers for fur (which was called 'Adelaide chinchilla'), and now affected by a disease called chlamydia which causes infertility.

Radio-Tracking Koalas

ARRGHH... THUD!

Wilcox

✰ **THE WOMBAT**, a marsupial, like a furry pig, which lives in a burrow.

✰ **THE PLATYPUS**, an egg-laying mammal called a monotreme (which means it uses the one hole for excretion, sex and egg laying) with the head and webbed feet of a duck and the furry body of an otter. It swims in the lakes and rivers of eastern Australia. When the first platypus was sent back to London, it was written off as a hoax. Now it's on the 20 cent coin.

✰ **THE ECHIDNA**, a monotreme with sharp spines, a long snout and a sticky tongue for catching insects. It's on the five cent coin.

✰ **THE BUDGERIGAR** is the best known of Australia's many parrots, and it became the world's most popular cage bird after a naturalist named John Gould took a breeding pair to England in 1840. In the 20th century several generations of Australian schoolchildren were forced to donate money to a charity called the Gould League of Bird Lovers.

✰ **THE KOOKABURRA** is a member of the kingfisher family, and comes in two types: the laughing jackass and the howling jackass (or blue-winged kookaburra). It laughs to warn other birds away from its territory.

✰ **THE FRILL-NECKED LIZARD** is one of about 400 lizard species in Australia, all of them harmless to humans. It puffs out its collar to frighten away predators.

☆ **THE DINGO**, a yellow wolf-like pest which is sometimes called 'the native dog', but which did not evolve on this continent. It is apparently a descendant of pets brought by settlers arriving from northern countries about 7000 years ago.

☆ **THE CANE TOAD** is not native to Australia but has become a figure in our folklore. It was brought from Hawaii to Australia's north-east coast in 1935 to eat beetles in the sugarcane fields. It ate everything except beetles, including small native animals. Its tough poisonous skin makes it impervious to most predators and it has now spread from Queensland west into the Northern Territory and south into New South Wales.

15
what we own

*W*e've golden soil and wealth for toil, says our national anthem. But we own only about two thirds of our soil. According to the latest information from the Bureau of Statistics: 'Of the total equity on issue by Australian enterprise groups at 30 June 1997, non-residents held equity valued at $214.3 billion (29 per cent) and residents held $529.8 billion (71 per cent).' The industries where foreign investment is highest are finance, manufacturing, and mining. The top overseas owner of Australia is the USA (22 per cent of foreign investment) followed by Britain (19 per cent) and Japan (13).

These are the main ways that Australia makes its wealth ... We receive 4 million foreign tourists a year (mainly from New Zealand, Japan, Britain and USA) who spend $16 billion. We sell coal (mainly to Japan and Korea) and earn $9.5 billion a year. We sell gold (mainly to Korea, Singapore and Hong Kong) and make $6.3 billion a year. We sell wheat all over the place and make $3.6 billion. And we sell iron ore (mainly to Japan, Korea and China) and make $3.8 billion.

These are the main ways we spend our wealth

overseas ... We import cars (mainly from Japan, Korea and Germany) at a cost of $6.5 billion. We import computers (mainly from the USA and Singapore) for $4.3 billion. We import oil (mainly from Indonesia, Vietnam and Papua New Guinea) for $3.3 billion. And we import telecommunications equipment (mainly from the USA and Japan) for $2.7 billion a year.

Australia spends more than it earns, so we have a balance of payments deficit of around $20 billion. And because our earnings depend so much on primary products (like coal and gold) which keep changing their value, we have to keep borrowing overseas. At the moment our net foreign debt amounts to around $200 billion (what we owe foreigners less what they owe us), of which a third is owed by governments and two thirds by private companies. If we add to that another $100 billion, which represents what foreigners own of us less what we own overseas, we could say that our real debt to the rest of the world is $300 billion.

Is this a problem? Yes, because we are living beyond our means, and sending much of our national wealth overseas as interest payments. What happens if we don't do anything about it? We'll all be poorer. What is the solution? For Australia to start manufacturing more complex products so we don't have to import them and can start selling them overseas. How do we go about this? I don't know.

16
the power structure

*i*n theory, the most powerful person in Australia is the governor-general, who is appointed by the Monarch of England to act as head of state. In practice, the Queen always accepts the recommendation of the prime minister on who should be governor-general, and the G-G is supposed to preside at ceremonial events and not interfere in the running of the country. The only recent exception to this principle was in 1975 when the G-G dismissed the prime minister because one of the houses of parliament would not pass his budget. At that point the governor-general was the most powerful person in Australia.

Most of the time, the most powerful person is the prime minister, who has the job because he or she is leader of the party with the most members elected to the House of Representatives. The House of Reps is theoretically the more important of the two houses of the national parliament. The other house, called the Senate, is supposed to represent the interests of Australia's states and territories. It has the power to block laws passed by the House of Reps, and does so often, causing the government to do a lot of arguing and sometimes amend the laws.

When the laws passed by the parliament are challenged, they are interpreted by the High Court of Australia. It is the court of final appeal for any Australian. So sometimes the High Court is the most powerful body in the country.

The High Court sits atop a pyramid of state and federal courts that make up the justice system. At the bottom are the state magistrates courts, which deal with minor offences or civil disputes over small amounts of money. More serious cases are tried before judges in District courts or judges and juries in Supreme courts. The losers in civil or criminal cases can seek help from the state court of appeal. Disputes involving federal laws are dealt with by federal courts. Divorce disputes over child custody or division of property are covered by the Family Court.

The federal government in Canberra collects income taxes, and is responsible for defence, foreign relations, and any problem of national concern. There are also six state governments and two territory governments responsible for such matters as police and schools. Every state has a governor, supposedly also the Queen's appointment but really the choice of the state premier, who is the head of the dominant party in the state parliament.

17
the parties

a ustralia has two main political parties: Liberal and Labor, and two minor ones: the Nationals and the Democrats. The Labor Party was founded by members of the trade union movement in 1891. They decided to spell the party's name without a 'u' because they felt stronger ties with American socialists than with their British comrades. The Liberal Party was founded in 1944 from 18 small anti-Labor organisations, primarily at the instigation of Robert Menzies. The Liberals operate in partnership with the National Party, which was originally called the Country Party, and was formed in 1920 by farming activists. This coalition was in power nationally from 1949 to 1972, then from 1975 to 1983, and was re-elected in 1996. In Queensland, the National Party is the dominant partner in the coalition.

Traditionally Liberal stood for big business, landlords and the rich while Labor stood for workers, tenants and the poor. From the 1970s, Labor stood for government intervention for social change while Liberal stood for letting business do what it liked. During the early 1990s, Liberal stood for constant change (of its leaders and policies) while Labor stood for whatever Paul Keating felt like on the day. In the late 1990s, the Liberal leader (and Prime Minister) is John Howard and the Labor leader (and Leader of the Opposition) is Kim Beazley.

And then there is the party called The Australian Democrats, which was formed in 1977 by Don Chipp, a disaffected Liberal, who thought the nation needed a party between Labor and Liberal to 'keep the bastards honest'. Its few parliamentary representatives are active on environmental issues and notorious for changing their minds. There is also a scattering of green representatives and independents in national and state parliaments who make the political process unpredictable and therefore interesting.

18
the republic

*t*he issue which has provoked the most public debate in Australia during the 1990s is whether we should sever our political ties with the British monarchy and become a republic. The Labor Party wants the King or Queen of England to cease being Australia's head of state, to be replaced by a locally chosen President. Its case has been helped by the behaviour of some members of the Royal Family in recent years. The National Party wants to retain ties with the monarchy, and the Liberal Party is divided on the issue, with the current Prime Minister, John Howard, leaning towards the Royals. Opinion polls show that just over half of the population favour a republic, with 70 per cent sure it is bound to happen eventually.

The problem is: how can the change be made with a minimum of fuss? If the governor-general is replaced by a president, should the president be elected by the people, chosen by a two thirds majority of the parliament, or appointed by the government? What powers should the president have to override the government? Would state governors have to be replaced by state presidents, and how would *they* be chosen? Could a state retain its ties with the British monarchy if the central government had severed them? Discussion continues. It does, however, seem unlikely that Prince Charles will ever be King of Australia.

19
states of origin

*j*udged on the way we vote with our feet, Queensland is the most popular state—its population swells by 45 000 every year. Victoria must be the least popular—it loses 25 000 people a year. Perhaps the secret lies in the slogans featured on the states' car licence plates.

Queensland calls itself 'The Sunshine State'. The Victorians used to call themselves 'The Garden State' then changed in the early 1990s to 'Victoria: On The Move'—which indeed they are (to Queensland). But the double meaning in the Victorian slogan wasn't nearly as embarrassing as the new slogan announced by the South Australian government in 1995. They decided to change from 'The Festival State' to 'SA: Going All The Way'. After complaints, the government made the new slogan optional.

Western Australia describes itself as 'The State of Excitement', presumably the prelude to going all the way, while Tasmania is comfortable with 'The Holiday Isle'. New South Wales is either boastful or historical with 'The First State', Canberra states the obvious with 'The Nation's Capital' and the Northern Territory, which would like to be a state but hasn't grown up enough yet, compensates by giving itself two slogans: 'Outback Australia' and 'Nature Territory'. In its advertising, it also asserts 'You'll never never know if you never never go', a reference to the uncharted bush area known as 'the Never Never'.

Here's a summary of other state differences:

☆ **NEW SOUTH WALES**. Population: 6 million. Capital: Sydney. Started as British penal colony in 1788. Emblem: the platypus or the kookaburra. Known for: police corruption, the Opera House.

☆ **QUEENSLAND**. Population: 3.4 million. Capital: Brisbane. Started as penal colony when Sydney was considered too civilised for convicts in 1825. Emblem: the koala. Known for: resort developers, pineapples.

☆ **VICTORIA**. Population: 4.5 million. Capital: Melbourne. Purchased by John Batman from local Aborigines for clothing, flour and tools in 1835 and declared a British colony in 1851. Emblem: the Leadbeater possum or the helmeted honeyeater (a bird). Known for: police shootings, the muddy Yarra River.

☆ **SOUTH AUSTRALIA**. Population: 1.5 million. Capital: Adelaide. Started by free settlers from England (no convict riff-raff) in 1836. Emblem: the hairy-nosed wombat. Known for: arts festivals, wine.

☆ **WESTERN AUSTRALIA**. Population: 1.7

million. Capital: Perth. Founded as a British military colony in 1829. Emblem: the numbat or the black swan. Known for: questionable millionaires, deserts.

☆ **TASMANIA**. Population: 465 000. Capital: Hobart. First claimed by Holland in 1642 and named Van Diemen's Land, then seized by the British for a penal colony in 1803. Emblem: the thylacine (Tasmanian tiger). Known for: apples, wildernesses.

☆ **NORTHERN TERRITORY**. Population: 200 000. Capital: Darwin. Part of NSW until 1863, then part of South Australia till 1911, then administered by the federal government. Emblem: the red kangaroo or the wedge-tailed eagle. Known for: beer drinking, crocodiles.

☆ **THE AUSTRALIAN CAPITAL TERRITORY**. Population: 300 000. Capital: Canberra. Land given by NSW to the federal government in 1911. Emblem: the gang gang cockatoo. Known for: public servants, planned suburbs.

Australia also administers seven external territories, including Norfolk Island (where Colleen McCullough lives), Cocos Island, Christmas Island and the Australian Antarctic Territory (where we claim 5.8 million square kilometres—nearly half of the frozen continent).

20

nine governments

*a*ustralia is the most governed nation on earth. For every 20 000 citizens, we have one full-time politician, and that's not counting all the local mayors and councillors. The British, who also consider themselves overgoverned, have one politician per 45 000 citizens. The reason Australia has so many pollies (and their accompanying bureaucrats) is that we have a national parliament and eight state or territory parliaments, most of which have two chambers. All of these governments not only cost a lot of money to run, but they waste a lot of time arguing about who has the power to do what.

One solution would be to abolish the state governments, and amalgamate Australia's 900 local councils into about 40 regional bodies, each responsible for about 500 000 people. The regional governments could deal with local concerns such as collecting the garbage and watering the parks, while the central government could run the country.

The current state boundaries were drawn up by British bureaucrats in the 19th century, and have no connection with geographical logic or regional identity. The people of far north Queensland feel just as separated from Brisbane as they do from

Canberra. They'd be better administered from Cairns. The town of Broome, on the Western Australian coast, has much more in common with Darwin than with Perth. Broken Hill is 500 kilometres from Adelaide and 1000 kilometres from Sydney, which officially runs it, and has more in common with Alice Springs.

If Australians are looking for a grand national transformation for the year 2001, to continue the momentum after we become a republic in 2000, there'd be no worthier project than the abolition of the states.

21
inventions

*a*ustralians are resourceful on a small scale. They tend to invent things they can knock together in the back shed rather than massive structures needing tedious research. Some examples of our triumphs ...

☆ **THE ALEXANDER TECHNIQUE.** A system of stress reduction by adjustment of posture was created in Melbourne by Frederick Alexander in the 1890s and is now taught round the world.

☆ **ASPRO.** A pain reliever based on aspirin was developed in 1917 by the Melbourne pharmacist George Nicholas, and by 1940 it was the world's most widely used headache treatment.

☆ **THE BIONIC EAR.** In 1978 a team led by Professor Graeme Clark of Melbourne University implanted a bundle of extremely fine electrodes into the ear of a man who had been made totally deaf by a car accident. After months of fine tuning he could hear again, and now a company called Cochlear Pty Ltd sells the technology to the world.

✩ **THE ESKY.** A company called Malley's sensed
the Australian need for a portable beer cooler
in 1950. They produced a steel box within a
steel box, and named it after the Eskimos. It
had a handle, a plug through which melted ice
could be drained off, and a bottle opener built
into the side. In the 1970s, the Esky became
plastic (letting us carry more beer).

✩ **THE STUMP JUMP PLOUGH.** In 1870, a
bolt broke in the plough Richard Smith was
using on rough land in Yorke Peninsula, South
Australia. He found that it moved more easily
over stumps and stones, so he went home and
perfected a 'pivoting ploughshare' that slid over
just the sort of land Australian farmers
encountered most often.

✩ **TEST-TUBE BABIES.** More babies from in-
vitro fertilisation have been born in Australia
than anywhere else, thanks to the work of
Professor Carl Wood at Monash University and
Dr Christopher Chen at Flinders Medical
Centre in Adelaide. We produced the world's
first test-tube twins (1981), triplets (1983),
quadruplets (1984), baby born from a donor
egg (1983) and frozen-embryo baby (1984).

✩ **ULTRASOUND.** Developed in 1961 by
scientists at the Commonwealth Health
Department, this method of testing the health
of unborn babies without the risk of X-rays is
now used around the world.

☆ **THE UTE.** In 1932, Lewis Brandt, a 22-year-old designer with the Ford company, drew up plans for a vehicle in which farmers could take the family to church on Sunday and the pigs to market on Monday. It came to be called the utility truck, or ute, although back in Detroit Henry Ford called it the 'kangaroo chaser'.

☆ **THE VICTA MOWER.** In 1952 in the Sydney suburb of Concord, Mervyn Victor Richardson welded a peach tin full of petrol to a miniature motor, and attached that to a lawn mower with rotary blades. The neighbours hated the sound but liked the results, and soon Mervyn was building hundreds of mowers in his backyard. He named his creation after his middle name. By the mid 1990s, six million Australians were turning grass into lawn with a Victa.

☆ **THE WINE CASK.** A plastic bag full of wine inside a cardboard box was developed by Thomas Angove, the head of a South Australian wine company, in 1967. Other wine companies have been improving on the tap, if not the contents, ever since.

☆ **ZINC CREAM.** Developed in the 1940s by the Fauldings pharmaceutical company, the white sunblock made from zinc oxide was saving Australians from skin cancer before they even knew there was a risk. In the 1980s Fauldings found a huge new market by producing it in colours and in sticks.

22
women

*i*t came as a surprise to Australian women when a United Nations Human Development Report in 1995 rated Australia fifth in the world among nations approaching equality between men and women. We had more in common with Finland than with Britain, which languished at number 13. We're behind Sweden, Finland, Norway and Denmark, equal fifth with America, and ahead of France, Japan, Canada and Austria.

The Gender Development Index is calculated on such measures as how women compare with men in income, life expectancy, adult literacy and school enrolments. If a score of 1 represents absolute equality, then Sweden scores 0.92, Australia and America score 0.90 and Austria scores 0.88. We're making progress. Back in 1970, we scored 0.72 while America scored 0.81.

But any measure of public power in Australia leaves women far behind. The United Nations ranks Australia well down in its table of female participation in Government decision-making. Only 15 per cent of our ministe-rial-level posts are held by women, compared with 38 per cent in Sweden, 24 per cent in Holland, 21 per cent in Ireland and 19 per cent in Canada. A similar figure emerges if you look at the propor-tion of women in the senior ranks of private enterprise.

The 'revolution' in women's roles, which has been one of the key transformations of Australian society since the 1960s, has a long way to go yet. The social researcher Hugh Mackay, in his book *Reinventing Australia*, portrays us as a nation of angry women and baffled men. More than 50 per cent of married women in Australia now have full-time jobs but, when they get home, they find they're still expected to be cleaner, cook and child raiser.

Mackay comments:

> The widespread failure of Australian men to adapt their behaviour to match the redefinition of gender roles which has taken place in the minds of Australian women represents another major source of anxiety for the working mother ... Recognising that his wife leads a very different kind of life from the one that she led 10 or 15 years ago (and a very different kind of life from the one his mother led), he clings to the hope that he might be able to maintain his existing pattern of living until the storm passes.

It's not surprising, then, that women now initiate most of the divorces in Australia.

23
tall poppies

*O*ne of Australia's healthiest national traits is the Tall Poppy Syndrome, which involves taking a sceptical view of people who are rich, powerful or successful, and cutting them down to size when they appear pretentious. It most likely originated in the convict era, when the only way the inmates of the open-air prison on Sydney Harbour could fight back at their jailers was to spread scurrilous gossip about them. Nowadays the ritual is most often directed at politicians, entrepreneurs and showbiz figures who go overseas and adopt American accents.

Victims of the syndrome say it is motivated by jealousy and a desire to perpetuate mediocrity. But Australians know it is unwise to make heroes too easily, since there's always the risk of later disappointment—as has happened to Americans, who are more inclined to engage in celebrity-worship.

Australians discarded the Tall Poppy Syndrome for a while in the mid 1980s, and let the media persuade them that a few business moguls were appropriate heroes, perhaps even better candidates for the job of national ruler than any of the politicians around at the time. By the early 1990s, those entrepreneurs were facing bankruptcy or stealing charges, or living permanently overseas, and Australians again realised the value of scepticism.

24

what makes us laugh

S ome reference points around which Australians build jokes . . .

☆ **MALCOLM FRASER'S TROUSERS.** One morning in October 1986, one of our most conservative former prime ministers was found wandering in a dazed condition through the lobby of a hotel in Memphis, Tennessee wearing a towel round his waist and no trousers. Fraser, in town for a conference, was apparently drugged and robbed by a lady he met in a bar.

☆ **BOB HAWKE'S ECCENTRICITIES.** As a union leader in the 1970s, Bob Hawke built up popularity as a knockabout Aussie bloke, notorious for drinking and womanising. He gave both up when he became Prime Minister in 1983, but developed the habit of crying on public occasions, such as when discussing his daughter's drug problem. After being displaced by Paul Keating in 1991, he hung around with some strange business types, divorced his wife Hazel after 40 years marriage, and married Blanche d'Alpuget, a journalist who had written his biography.

☆ **PAULINE HANSON'S POLICIES.** A former Liberal Party member and fish and chip shop owner, Hanson ('the redhead for the rednecks') won the Queensland seat of Oxley as an Independent in 1996 on a platform of ending Asian immigration and eliminating assistance to Aborigines. She founded a right wing party called One Nation, but lost her seat in the 1998 election.

☆ **MAL COLSTON'S EXPENSES.** Formerly a Labor Party senator, Colston turned into an independent senator voting with the Liberal Party, and then came under investigation over his enormous claims for travel expenses, which he blamed on his secretary's inefficiency.

☆ **BRIAN HARRADINE'S INFLUENCE.** A Catholic conservative from Tasmania, Harradine held the balance of power in the Senate, so the Government was always happy to heed his views on contraception, abortion and censorship.

☆ **JEFF KENNETT'S ARROGANCE.** The Premier of Victoria is regularly ridiculed by those outside his State for his pompadour hairdo, his aggressive manner, and his one-eyed fervour for all things Victorian.

☆ **GRAHAM RICHARDSON'S DEVIOUSNESS.** Richardson was a Labor Party organiser famous for combining charm with pressure to achieve agreement on policy changes. In his 1994 book, *Whatever It Takes*, he argued that in politics, lying is an acceptable tactic for a

worthy goal. He is now a lobbyist for
Australia's richest man, Kerry Packer.

☆ **DINGOES**. After a baby named Azaria
Chamberlain disappeared at Ayers Rock in
1980, apparently seized by a dingo, Australians
could not resist creating sick jokes on the subject.
For example . . . 'Q. What do you call a child in
a pram at Ayers Rock? A. Meals on wheels.' Etc.

☆ **CHRISTOPHER SKASE'S ILLNESS**. Australia's
most famous fugitive is Christopher Skase, a
1980s entrepreneur who left the country in 1991
owing huge debts and went to live in Spain.
During an extradition hearing, he convinced a
Spanish court that he was too sick to be flown
home by appearing each day in a wheelchair and
sucking on an oxygen mask for emphysema.

☆ **ALAN BOND'S MEMORY**. Australia's most
famous amnesiac is Alan Bond, another 1980s
entrepreneur who suffered constant memory
loss while being questioned during bankruptcy
and fraud hearings.

☆ **THE WHITE SHOE BRIGADE**. Generic name
for a species of Queensland businessman who
seems able to bypass environmental restrictions
to build resort and shopping developments by
reason of a close relationship with certain
government ministers. Often discussed in
association with Joh Bjelke-Petersen, a
pro-development Premier of Queensland
famous for his contorted mode of speech.

☆ **PAUL KEATING'S TONGUE**. As Treasurer during the 1980s and as Prime Minister during the 1990s, Keating was just too clever for his own good. Notorious for his short temper and abusive language, he enraged Australians by warning them that their laziness could produce a 'banana republic', by telling them that a recession in the early 1990s was 'the correction we had to have' and by publicly complaining that he didn't know what Australians were 'on about' when they doubted his boasts about an economic recovery. He lost office in 1996.

☆ **MEN**. A special genre of joke, told mostly by Australian women, has developed around the Aussie male's image of selfishness, sexism and heavy drinking. Q. What's an Australian man's idea of foreplay? A. Are you awake, love? Q. Why is an Australian man so quick when having sex? A. So he can get to the pub and tell his mates about it.

25
the weather

*a*ustralia is a land of climatic extremes, wherein one area can be ravaged by drought at the same time as other parts are under flood. There have been nine major droughts in the past 150 years, with the worst one, between 1895 and 1903, affecting the whole continent and killing half the sheep and cattle around at the time.

Melbourne has the reputation as Australia's wettest capital, but that's a myth Australians are reluctant to give up. In fact, Hobart averages the most rainy days (159 a year) with Melbourne second (147). If we're talking about quantities of water rather than regular drizzle, the wettest capital is Darwin (1659 millimetres annual rainfall), with sunny Sydney second (1223 millimetres).

Darwin is also the hottest city (averaging 29

degrees in mid summer and 25 in what passes for winter) with Perth coming second, while the coldest capital is Canberra (from 20 degrees in summer to 5 in winter) with Hobart a close second. Canberra is also our foggiest capital, which is suitably symbolic, while Perth is our windiest.

The hottest place in Australia is Marble Bar, in Western Australia, which averages 41 degrees in summer. The coldest place is Charlotte's Pass, in the Snowy Mountains of New South Wales, where a temperature of minus 22 degrees has twice been recorded.

And while we're talking myths about weather, the Bureau of Meteorology wants to put on record that its forecasts are right more often than they are wrong—85 per cent of the time, in fact. They say that, on average, their temperature predictions for the capital cities are out by 1.5 degrees (while in the 1970s, they used to be out by 2 degrees).

So we'd better trust them when they suggest that Australia's weather will be getting hotter and sunnier over the next few years. We'll be affected by the general warming of the planet's atmosphere, and we'll be particular victims of the ragged holes that keep appearing in the protective ozone layer over the southern hemisphere, caused by chlorine from the chemicals the world produces. So the image of future Australians will need to include sunglasses, big hats and strong sunblock creams.

26
the explorers

*t*he first hundred years after white settlement in Australia was a period of frantic journeying, as the whites tried to establish what kind of continent they'd got themselves into. The key names in these epic and often foolhardy expeditions were . . .

☆ **MATTHEW FLINDERS.** Between 1795 and 1801 he mapped the bays and rivers south of Sydney, sailed round Tasmania to confirm that it was an island, and then sailed round the entire Australian coastline. He was the first to promote the name Terra Australis or Australia.

☆ **WILLIAM CHARLES WENTWORTH.** In 1813, with Lawson and Blaxland, he made the first crossing by white people of the Blue Mountains west of Sydney. He became a campaigner for political reforms such as trial by jury and an elected Legislative Council, which turned into the system of parliamentary democracy.

☆ **JOHN OXLEY.** Appointed Surveyor-General of NSW in 1812, he explored most of the state, mapping the Lachlan, Macquarie, Tweed and Brisbane Rivers.

☆ **HAMILTON HUME AND WILLIAM HOVELL.** In 1824 they journeyed south from Sydney, crossed the Murrumbidgee and Murray Rivers, and reached what became the site of Melbourne.

☆ **THOMAS MITCHELL.** He followed Oxley as Surveyor-General in 1828, planned the main roads around Sydney, figured out the river system of southern NSW, and mapped much of Victoria. He introduced a policy of using Aboriginal place names instead of echoing British towns and dignitaries.

☆ **CHARLES STURT.** In the 1820s he explored the river systems of NSW and, in 1844, he set off from Adelaide in search of the inland sea in the centre of the continent. He didn't find it.

☆ **LUDWIG LEICHHARDT.** In 1845 he mapped the top of Australia from north Queensland to the Northern Territory, and in 1848 he set out to cross the continent from east to west. He never returned. Patrick White's book *Voss* is about the madness of the European explorer in the desert.

☆ **EDWARD JOHN EYRE.** In 1840 he travelled from Adelaide along the Great Australian Bight to Albany, Western Australia.

☆ **ROBERT BURKE AND WILLIAM WILLS.** In 1861 they set off from Melbourne and crossed the continent from south to north, but died in Queensland on the return journey.

☆ **JOHN McDOUALL STUART**. In 1862 he
crossed the continent from Adelaide to the
Northern Territory, mapping the route for the
first overland telegraph line.

☆ **ERNEST GILES**. In 1875 he crossed the
continent from east to west, using camels, and
opened up much of central Australia for further
exploration.

27
sites and sights

*a*ustralians have a great tradition of building Big Creatures all over the landscape, with the hope of attracting jaded tourists to otherwise uninspiring districts. At last count, there were more than 60 giant replicas around the continent, including the Big Banana (Coffs Harbour, NSW), the Big Lobster (Kingston, SA), the Big Pineapple (Nambour, Qld), the Big Merino (Goulburn, NSW), the Big Apple (Donnybrook, Western Australia), the Big Crocodile (Larrimah, NT), the Big Bull (Wauchope, NSW) and the Big Ned Kelly (Glenrowan, Victoria).

This edifice complex is puzzling, considering that the continent has so many natural spectacles to inspire our awe. Here's a selection of more enduring wonders . . .

☆ **THE GREAT BARRIER REEF.**
The largest and most complex living coral system in the world, it stretches 2300 kilometres along the

Queensland coast. It's possible to explore the reef from resort towns such as Cairns, or from islands on the reef, such as Dunk, Hayman, Heron or Magnetic.

☆ **AYERS ROCK AND THE OLGAS.** About 500 kilometres south-west of Alice Springs, the changing reds of Uluru (Ayers Rock) and the pitted domes of Kata Tjuta (the Olga mountains) have eerie power.

☆ **KAKADU NATIONAL PARK.** Three hours drive from Darwin, Australia's largest national park offers lakes, waterfalls, 275 bird species and ancient Aboriginal rock art, particularly at Nourlangie. It's classified by UNESCO as a World Heritage Area.

☆ **THE GREAT OCEAN ROAD.** For 300 kilometres along the southern coastline of Victoria, the road winds round surfing beaches, over clifftops, through rainforests and past bizarre rock formations such as The Twelve Apostles, 100-metre-tall pillars thrusting out of the sea.

☆ **SHARK BAY.** About 800 kilometres north of Perth, on the central coast of Western Australia near Carnarvon, you can swim with dolphins at a beach called Monkey Mia, examine 3500-million-year old fossils around Hamelin Pool, and stand on the spot where Dirck Hartog, one of the earliest European visitors to Australia, nailed a pewter plate to a tree.

☆ **CRADLE MOUNTAIN.** In the middle of Tasmania's wilderness, Cradle Mountain is one of eight areas in Australia classified as world heritage by UNESCO, and offers some of Australia's grandest scenery.

☆ **FRASER ISLAND.** The world's largest sand island, off the Queensland coast 200 kilometres north of Brisbane, it contains lakes, dense rainforest and multicoloured sand cliffs.

28
Ned Kelly

*i*t's a bit of a mystery how a thief and murderer like Edward Kelly managed to capture the imagination of Australians. Perhaps it was the suit of armour he wore, which made him look like a walking letter box. Perhaps it was his self-image as an Australian Robin Hood, helping the poor of his district and resisting brutal authority figures. Perhaps it was his claim that he became a bush-ranger because he was a victim of the historic oppression of Irish Catholics by English Protestants. Those three elements have somehow combined to make Edward Kelly a central symbol in our bush mythology.

The son of an Irish convict, he grew up on farms in northern Victoria and started his crime career at the age of 15 with a conviction for assault in 1870,

Look, madam, I may be a hero, but I can't guarantee next day delivery

followed by a three-year jail sentence for horse stealing in 1871. With his brother Dan he formed a gang which robbed travellers and banks and, in 1878, the gang shot dead three policemen sent to arrest them.

Then they took over the town of Jerilderie and held the population hostage in the Royal Mail Hotel. Kelly dictated a long letter in which he described himself as a political activist against the oppression of the Irish. He said he could no longer 'put up with the brutal and cowardly conduct of a parcel of big ugly fat-necked wombat headed big bellied magpie legged narrow hipped splay footed sons of Irish bailiffs of English landlords'.

In June 1880 the Kelly gang forced railway workers to tear up the railway lines that were to bring a train full of police reinforcements to the town of Glenrowan. The police got there anyway, and Kelly was finally wounded and captured after a shootout. He was convicted of murder and hanged in Melbourne Jail on 11 November 1880, at the age of 25. His last words were either 'Such is life' or 'Ah well, I suppose it has come to this'.

29
what puzzles us

a ustralia's biggest unsolved mysteries are:

☆ **BOGLE–CHANDLER**. The partly clothed
bodies of Gilbert Bogle, a CSIRO scientist, and
Margaret Chandler, a nurse married to another
CSIRO scientist, were found on the banks of
Sydney's Lane Cove River early on New Year's
Day, 1963. The cause of death was apparently
poisoning, but what the poison was, and who
administered it, remain unknown. A popular
theory is that Bogle was doing secret drug
experiments for the CIA, and may have been
killed by enemy (or even friendly) agents.

☆ **AZARIA CHAMBERLAIN**. On 17 August
1980, a nine-week-old baby named Azaria
Chamberlain disappeared from a tent at a
campsite near Ayers Rock in central Australia.
Her mother Lindy said she thought she had
seen a dingo dragging something away. The
child's clothes were later found in a cave. Two
years later, Lindy Chamberlain was convicted
of murdering the child and sentenced to life
imprisonment, while her husband Michael was

convicted of being an accessory. She spent three years in jail but, after an inquiry, her conviction was overturned.

☆ **HAROLD HOLT.** The Prime Minister of Australia went for a swim in heavy surf at Portsea, south of Melbourne, on 17 December 1967. He has not been seen in Australia since. One theory is that he was picked up by a Chinese submarine and went on to direct a Chinese espionage program against Australia.

☆ **MR CRUEL.** On the evening of 13 April 1991, Karmein Chan, 13, was abducted from her home at Templestowe, Melbourne. The abductor, thought to have been responsible for at least ten other abductions, assaults and rapes in Melbourne, was named 'Mr Cruel' by the media. Police have no suspects.

☆ **THE WANDA BEACH MURDERS.** The bodies of two 15-year-old girls, Christine Sharrock and Marianne Schmidt, were found in a shallow grave on Sydney's Wanda Beach on 12 January 1965. They had gone for a stroll along the sand after a picnic with friends. They had been stabbed to death. Police still have no suspects.

☆ **THE TASMANIAN TIGER.** Every few years an adventurer mounts an expedition through the wilderness of Tasmania in search of an animal technically known as the thylacine. These 'tigers' roamed the whole Australian continent ten thousand years ago, but were hunted to near extinction first by the Aborigines and then by white farmers trying to protect their sheep. The last confirmed thylacine died in Hobart Zoo in 1936. But, if you're tempted, you should look for a large wolf with yellow fur and dark stripes around its back.

30
births

*h*oo-wah, they're at it like bunnies in the Northern Territory, while in Canberra they'd rather talk politics. That's one way to interpret the current pattern of births in Australia. The Australian Bureau of Statistics reported in 1995 that the Northern Territory had the highest fertility rate of all regions of the country, while Canberra had the lowest, thereby disposing of the theory that power is the ultimate aphrodisiac.

The ABS defines fertility rate as 'the number of children one woman would expect to bear during her child bearing lifetime', and says the NT figure is 2.3, Canberra's is 1.7 and the national average is 1.8.

Australia's fertility figure makes us comparable with cold countries like Britain, Holland and Canada, which are all behind the ideal replacement rate of 2.1. We're far behind such warm nations as Egypt (4.2), Papua New Guinea (4.9) and the Philippines (4.0).

About 253 000 children are born each year in Australia, and about 26

per cent of them are to unmarried women (compared with 15 per cent in the early 1980s). Again the Northern Territory scores highest on this measure (55 per cent unmarried) while respectable Victoria scores lowest (20 per cent).

Women are waiting longer to have children. The median age of new mothers is now 29, compared with 27 in the early 1980s. The median age of first fathers is 32, also two years older than in the early 1980s. It also seems that Australian men are becoming more honest and responsible. Back in 1983, 36 per cent of male partners in what the Bureau of Stats calls 'exnuptial births' refused to acknowledge parenthood, while in the 1990s, only 18 per cent of unmarried fathers are putting up an argument.

And when are Australians at their most active? More babies are born in March than any other month (conceived in winter) while babies are least likely to be born in November (conceived in March). So much for the languid sweaty sensuousness of summer.

31
names

*W*hat Australians call their children has changed noticeably over the years, so that the name of someone you're introduced to can be a useful clue to age. A person called Sky or Rainbow was probably born in the late 1960s. A woman called Susan is in her mid 30s. A man called Adam is in his mid 20s. Anyone called Jason or Kylie was born in the mid 1970s or else in the late 1980s (after 'Neighbours' became our national soap opera). Kylie, by the way, is alleged to be an Aboriginal word for boomerang and, indeed, she does keep coming back.

But let's be scientific about this. Here is a table of most popular baby names, based on the birth notices in Sydney newspapers over the past four decades.

First the girls . . .

☆ **THE 1950s:** Ann(e), Margaret, Elizabeth, Jennifer, Mary.
☆ **THE 1960s:** Jennifer, Julie, Catherine, Leanne, Kerry.
☆ **THE 1970s:** Sarah, Nicole, Michelle, Rebecca, Belinda.

☆ **THE 1980s:** Sarah, Katherine, Jessica, Rebecca, Elizabeth.
☆ **THE 1990s:** Emma, Madeleine, Jessica, Sophie, Emily.

And now the boys . . .

☆ **THE 1950s:** John, David, James, Peter, William.
☆ **THE 1960s:** Mark, David, Peter, Paul, Michael.
☆ **THE 1970s:** Andrew, David, Matthew, Michael, Christopher.
☆ **THE 1980s:** Andrew, James, David, Matthew, Michael.
☆ **THE 1990s:** James, Thomas, Alexander, Matthew, Benjamin.

Of course, if any of these kids happened to have red hair, they'd be nicknamed Blue or Bluey, unless they were called Ginger Meggs (an Australian comic-strip character since the 1930s). A child with dark hair might get Snowy, and a tall child might get Shorty, unless he was called Lofty. Australian nick-naming usually operates on the principle of opposites, but not always.

32
the way of death

*W*e're healthier than the English, the New Zealanders and the Americans, but sicker than the French, the Japanese and the Swedish, as measured by our life expectancy (which is 75 for a boy born in 1995 and 81 for a girl born in 1995). About 129 000 Australians die every year. For women over 35, the biggest killers are heart disease followed by cancer. For men over 35, the killers are cancer followed by heart disease. Around 400 people—97 per cent of them male—die each year from disorders connected with AIDS.

For people under 35, the biggest killers are accidents, with men four times more likely to be involved in one than women. Of the 7 500 deaths not caused by disease each year, around 32 per cent are caused by suicide (mainly men), 27 per cent are caused by car crashes, and 4.5 per cent are caused by murder (also mainly men).

But a detailed look at the death statistics produces a number of puzzles. What, for example, do we make of

the facts that more of this country's deaths happen in August than any other month, and that Canberra has the lowest death rate of all the capital cities, but the highest rate of male suicides? And among Australians born overseas, why would the Vietnamese have the highest suicide rate (87 per 100 000), followed by New Zealanders (53) while the Italians have the lowest (12)? And what's so special about Queensland that women are less likely to die there than in any other state?

There is no mystery, however, about why the Northern Territory has the highest death rate—it has the largest Aboriginal population. In the Northern Territory, 49 per cent of deaths (and 73 per cent of infant deaths) are of indigenous people, even though they make up only 23 per cent of the territory's population. The assumptions about life expectancy I mentioned at the beginning don't apply to the original Australians, who might as well be living in the Third World—the life expectancy for an Aboriginal woman is 59, and for an Aboriginal man it's 53.

33
family life

*C*ontrary to our self-image as a land of mum-dad-and-two-kiddies households, Australia is becoming a land of lonely soloists, broken marriages and homes where the grown-up kids refuse to leave. The Bureau of Statistics reports that, way back in 1976, 60 per cent of Australian households contained couples with children. By 1998, this figure had fallen to 42 per cent, because of the growth of one-parent families and childless couples. About 40 per cent of first marriages now end in divorce. Those couples who stay together to let the kids reach adulthood find they can't get rid of them—40 per cent of Australians aged between 20 and 24 now live with their parents, compared with 34 per cent in the mid 1980s.

There are 106 000 marriages a year in Australia, and 52 000 divorces, so we have the world's third highest divorce rate (after the US and UK). Until 1976, Australian divorce law required that one spouse had to prove the other

'at fault' in some way—guilty of infidelity, for example. Since the Family Law Act of 1976, the only grounds for divorce is 'irretrievable breakdown' of the marriage, which can be established by the couple living apart for at least 12 months. This put a lot of private detectives out of work.

Divorce is becoming more fashionable. Between 1995 and 1996, the latest available statistics, the number of divorced people grew by 4 per cent (to 900 000) while the general adult population rose by 1.2 per cent (to 14 million). Australia now has 396 000 divorced men and 504 000 divorced women.

Faced with these breakdown statistics, people seem to be thinking longer before they marry. More than half the people who marry in Australia live together first. The average age of first marriage is now 29 for men, compared with 23 in the early 1970s, and 26 for women, compared with 21. So people are marrying later and divorcing earlier— nearly 50 per cent of divorces happen within the first ten years of marriage. Apparently they want to be sure they're young enough to try again. But men find it easier than women. The male remarriage rate is 54 per thousand, while the female remarriage rate is 24 per thousand.

34
our wars

a ustralians have been involved in all the big wars of the 20th century, usually helping out other nations rather than defending their own country. We joined Britain in fighting the Boer War in Africa and lost 588 soldiers between 1899 and 1902. Then we joined Britain in fighting World War One in Europe and the Middle East, losing 60 454 soldiers between 1914 and 1918. The most remembered campaign was the failure at Gallipoli, which gave us the Anzac legend.

In 1939 we joined Britain in fighting World War Two in Europe, then realised we were more endangered in the Pacific, especially in February 1942 when 188 Japanese aircraft attacked Darwin, killing 243 people. Over the next two years Darwin was bombed 57 times. There were air attacks on northern coastal towns in Western Australia and Queensland, and underwater attacks on Newcastle and Sydney in May and June 1942 by Japanese midget submarines (one of which sank a ship called the *Kuttabul*, killing 17 naval ratings).

The World War Two equivalent of the Gallipoli legend was the Kokoda Trail in New Guinea, where Australian troops fought disease and dense jungle in

September 1942, to prevent the Japanese reaching Port Moresby. In all, Australia lost 39 429 soldiers between 1939 and 1945.

Next we joined Britain in fighting communist rebels in Malaya and Borneo, and lost 54 soldiers between 1948 and 1966. We lost 339 fighting for the USA and South Korea in the Korean War between 1950 and 1953, and 496 fighting for the USA and South Vietnam in the Vietnam War between 1963 and 1972. In 1991 we sent navy ships and 1631 people to support the USA and Kuwait in the Gulf War, and lost nobody.

35
the images we love

S ome insight into the symbols Australians hold dearest can be gained from a survey conducted in 1995 by the *Sydney Morning Herald*'s 'Stay in Touch' column. The column asked readers to nominate the national icons which should be commemorated on stamps, and these got the most votes: 1 Vegemite 2 Akubra hat and Drizabone 3 meat pie and sauce 4 a lifesaver and surf-reel 5 Hills Hoist 6 the Sydney Harbour Bridge and Opera House 7 Uluru (Ayers Rock) 8 a Holden car 9 a glass or can of beer 10 a lamington.

Each of these icons has a chapter of its own in this book. Some of the other symbols frequently nominated were:

☆ **AEROPLANE JELLY.**
These packets of coloured crystals were first marketed in 1927, and advertised on radio with a jingle thought to be written by the company's founder Bert Appleroth (but more likely by a music-hall

pianist called Alfred Lenertz). All Australians over 30 should know it by heart:

'I like Aeroplane Jelly, Aeroplane Jelly for me. I like it for dinner, I like it for tea. A little each day is a good recipe. The quality's high as the name will imply. And it's made from pure fruit, one more good reason why I like Aeroplane Jelly, Aeroplane Jelly for me.'

☆ **A GRANNY SMITH APPLE.** This long-lasting green apple, now one of the world's most marketed varieties (because it takes a long time to go rotten), supposedly appeared by accident in 1868, when Maria Smith threw some Tasmanian apple cores into her garden at Eastwoood, Sydney.

☆ **ARNOTT'S BISCUITS.** Developed in the 1860s by an immigrant Scottish pastrycook named William Arnott, they became Australia's dominant brand. In the early 1990s, the company was taken over by an American multinational. The varieties with maximum nostalgia value are Iced Vo Vos, Adora Cream Wafers, Saos, Nice, Jatz and Milk Arrowroot.

☆ **A DIDGERIDOO.** A decorated hollow tube of wood which amplifies the sound of lips and voice when used by an Aboriginal musician.

☆ **GARDEN SWANS.** Made from peeled-back car tyres, painted white.

☆ **BANANAS IN PYJAMAS.** Two characters, known as B1 and B2, in an ABC television children's series whose associated products have given the ABC a marketing bonanza.

Some contributors took a more cynical view in their suggestions for typically Australian phenomena suitable for representation on stamps: the dole queue, melanoma, Aboriginal deaths in custody, a mortgage, a property developer, drought, a yobbo spewing in a gutter, water pollution, the White Australia Policy, and logging in native forests.

In the end, the post office declined all the suggestions from the *Sydney Morning Herald*'s readers, and issued a stamp series on Australian movies.

36
Vegemite

a black spread made from the yeasty waste products of beer manufacture plus a lot of salt would not seem a highly marketable proposition at first sight. It was the brainchild of a Victorian food entrepreneur named Fred Walker, who launched it in 1923 in a cylindrical jar with the subtitle 'pure vegetable extract'. He promoted it as a children's health food with an advertising jingle that told how, 'happy little Vegemites' would eat the product 'for breakfast lunch and tea' and ended with the claim that it 'puts a rose in every cheek'.

In 1935, Walker's company was bought by the Kraft cheese conglomerate, and Australia's own spread has been 100% American-owned ever since.

Somehow Vegemite managed to become such a national addiction that many Australians travelling overseas slip a couple of jars into their bags for fear it will be unavailable in less civilised nations. In an attempt to appear conscious of modern health concerns, the manufacturers recently reduced the salt content from 10 per cent to 8 per cent, but no matter how thinly you spread it, it's still too salty.

37
hats and coats

a kubra hats are the only known use for the rabbits that were introduced into Australia in 1859 so that an English squire living in Victoria could feel at home. The rabbits proceeded to breed and burrow under the entire nation so rampantly that, in the late 1940s, the CSIRO had to start spreading a disease called myxomatosis which killed millions of them without affecting native wildlife.

The rabbit plague would have been even worse if it had not been for an English immigrant named Benjamin Dunkerly, who set up as a fur cutter in Tasmania in 1872, and started using rabbits to make broad-brimmed bush hats. The hats came to be called Akubras, from an Aboriginal word for head covering. About seven rabbit skins go into each hat, so as Dunkerly's business spread to the mainland, he provided a valuable extermination service.

As a fashion item, Akubras are usually worn with large oilskin coats called Drizabones (made by an English-owned company). These were modelled on wet-weather gear worn by sailors last century, and designed to be loose enough to cover both horse and rider in a rainstorm. They have become part of Australia's stereotype as a rural nation, and most wearers these days have never slapped thigh to horse in their lives.

And back to the rabbits for a moment. They have reached plague proportions again, and the CSIRO is using a new control method called Rabbit Calicivirus Disease, which induces respiratory failure. In October 1996, infected rabbits were set free to spread the bad news in 400 sites across the country. Just to make sure they weren't about to encounter a public outcry about cruelty to sweet little bunnies, the CSIRO did a survey of Australian attitudes. It turns out that 96 per cent of us say rabbits are pests that must be controlled (that's six per cent more than the proportion of Australians who knew in 1996 that the Olympics will be held in Sydney in the year 2000). So we are not a nation of bunny lovers. Of course, if every Australian wore an Akubra, the calicivirus would not be necessary.

38
the meat pie

*t*he American invaders Ronald McDonald and
Colonel Sanders have made large inroads into our
fast food habits, but they haven't caught up with Australia's traditional takeaway—the meat pie. The
passion goes back at least 150 years. In 1869, Marcus
Clarke, then visiting from England, wrote about the
pie stalls of Bourke Street, Melbourne, where a
pieman poked a hole in the crust with his finger and
poured in a 'gravy' of salt and water (this being before
the development of tomato sauce in the 1880s). A
fellow customer reassured
Clarke about the contents:
'Mutton's cheaper than cat'.

These days around 260
million of these mystery
bags are consumed every
year, with demand peaking
in August. The passion is
not evenly distributed
among the population. A
survey by the Meat and
Livestock Corporation in
1995 found that men eat
nearly twice as many as

women (men average 2.9 a month, women 1.9) with males aged 18–35 averaging four a month.

Chopped steak is the filling in 62 per cent of pies eaten in Australia, followed in popularity by steak and onion, steak and kidney, steak and potato, and steak and mushroom. The poor old chicken pie manages a mere 2 per cent of the market.

The vast majority of meat pies are consumed with tomato sauce. Adelaide consumers are unique in the nation for their habit of surrounding their steak pies in pea soup, calling them 'floaters'. Queenslanders eat the most pies (averaging 2.5 a month) while Western Australians eat the least (1.3). NSW people have a particular preference for steak and mushroom.

Asked how they would like to improve the national dish, the Australians surveyed gave two answers most often: 'I'd like to know more about what's in them' and 'less gristle'. Female consumers tended to the first comment, and Western Australians the second, which may explain their low consumption figures.

39
surf and skin

*S*ince Australia is really a beach culture rather than a bush culture, it's important that the populace has some protection against large waves, strong undertows and its own foolishness. The world's first lifesaving club was founded at Bondi Beach, Sydney on 6 February 1906. Its members were a bunch of keen bodysurfers who got together to fight a law, originally passed in 1838, that forbade ocean bathing in daylight on the grounds of public decency. They won their battle, the law was revoked, and they then set about rescuing those who were too reckless with their newfound freedom.

Later that year the club captain, Lyster Ormsby, invented the lifesaving reel, a belt which went round the lifesaver's waist, attached to a rope around a giant wooden reel which could be wound in when the lifesaver had grabbed the endangered swimmer. Since then, Bondi's lifesavers have rescued 400 000 people. There are now 260 lifesaving clubs across Australia, with membership totalling 73 000, and they rescue 11 000 people a year.

We're almost as good at surfboard riding as we are at lifesaving. Our passion started in 1915 when a Hawaiian swimming champion named Duke Kahanamoku demonstrated board riding at Sydney's Freshwater Beach. Since then the boards have got smaller and the legends have got bigger. The first official world surfing championship, held at Manly, Sydney in 1964, was won by an Australian, Bernard 'Midget' Farrelly. Other world champions we remember: Nat Young (1970), Mark Richards (1979–82), Tom Carroll (1983, 1984) and Pam Burridge (1990).

But while we are well protected against drowning, we don't protect ourselves so well against another danger at our beaches—the sun. Australia has the world's highest rate of a potentially fatal skin cancer called melanoma: 5 per 100 000 men and 2 per 100 000 women, compared with a rate of 2 and 1 in Hawaii, where you'd imagine they'd be just as surf-crazy as us. Australians are gradually learning to stay out of the sun between midday and 2 p.m. and to wear hats and maximum sunblock the rest of the time.

40
the Hills Hoist

*i*n 1946, Lance Hill, a car mechanic newly returned from the war to his Adelaide home, wanted to make washing day easier for his wife. His aim was to construct a clothesline which could hold a double sheet and a lot of smalls, and be low enough for a short person to reach, yet high enough to catch the breeze. Of course, it had to be circular, mounted on a pole, able to rotate and be raised and lowered with a crank handle. And able to survive tornados and lightning strikes.

For the raising mechanism, he used a modified form of a car differential. He welded the whole thing together with pipes in the laundry, and when the neighbours saw how well it worked, they all wanted one. Lance and his brother-in-law went into business, and opened a factory in 1948. Lance Hill died a multimillionaire in 1986, aged 83, happily surveying an Australian landscape full of hoisted backyards. In the early 1990s, his factory cele-brated the millionth hoist off the production line. These days the Hills

company offers smaller, trendier variations with names like the Foldaline and the Quickdry, but nothing matches the original for durability—as anyone foolish (and unpatriotic) enough to try to remove a Hills Hoist from a backyard will quickly learn.

41
the coathanger

*i*t seems unfair that Sydney is overendowed with landmarks, while Melbourne has none. But the Melburnians have only themselves to blame. In the early 1980s they held a competition to design an inspiring structure that would make the city skyline memorable, but they couldn't agree on a winner.

When Sydney ran its design competition in 1955 for an opera house to stand on the site of an old tram terminus at Bennelong Point, the judges had no trouble throwing out 232 other entries and agreeing on the vision of a Danish architect named Joern Utzon. They thought the complex looked like a set of sails, which was ideal for the harbour setting. Utzon said later he was inspired by a pile of orange segments.

The trouble came when the builders tried to turn Utzon's sketches into a practical structure for concerts, plays, operas and meetings. The arguments that ensued led to Utzon's resignation from the project. The building took six years to construct and turned out pretty well from the outside, but too cramped inside for the comfort of performers and stage hands.

Back in 1932, the Sydney Harbour Bridge also

opened with a touch of disappointment. When construction started in 1922, it was planned to be the world's longest single-span bridge, but as Sydney's masterpiece was nearing completion, New York City unveiled a new coathanger that was 63 centimetres longer. Still, Sydney's bridge has pylons, and can carry far more weight than New York's Bayonne. And it met Sydney's traffic needs until the early 1990s, when an underwater tunnel was added to relieve the burden—just around the time the NSW government finished paying off the debt on the bridge.

42
Uluru

t he huge red rock in the middle of Australia was discovered by Aboriginal people some 40 000 years ago, and named Uluru by the local tribes. In 1873 a white man named William Gosse, who was trying to travel from Alice Springs to Perth, climbed the rock and named it after Sir Henry Ayers, a former Premier of South Australia. Aboriginal title to the rock was acknowledged by the Australian government in the 1980s, and it is now leased from the local tribes and treated as a tourist resort.

Geologists will tell you Uluru is actually a monadnock, meaning an isolated hill of rock that stands above the surrounding country. The world's largest monolith measures 3.1 kilometres east to west, 1.9 kilometres north to south, 348 metres in height, and 9.4 kilometres around.

Nearly 300 000 people visit it each year, but they don't realise the risk they are taking. As well as being our most famous natural feature, Uluru is our most dangerous. *The Medical Journal of Australia* reported that

95

between mid 1991 and the end of 1992, the Ayers Rock Medical Centre treated 255 injuries classified as serious (life threatening or needing more than 90 minutes treatment). There were 13 heart attacks suffered by people trying to climb the Rock, and six deaths—three from heart attacks, one suicide and two from car accidents. The incidence of heart attacks for people aged 25–69 is 7.2 per thousand per year at Uluru, while the Australian average is 2.45 per thousand per year.

So the place is a menace. And we're not even counting the risk of having your baby taken by a dingo.

43
Holdens, etc

*i*n the mid 1950s, a Melbourne housewife named Edna Everage made this comment: 'I think General Motors are absolutely marvellous, don't you? I mean, letting us call it "Australia's own car". They didn't have to do that. Such a wonderful gesture.' Edna, who is the alter ego of the comedian Barry Humphries, was talking about a car called the Holden. She was voicing the irony many Australians felt in the fact that the first mass-produced 'all-Australian car', named after the local car dealer Sir Edward Holden and launched with great fanfare from a Melbourne factory in 1948, had been designed in America, and most of the profits from its sales flew across the Pacific to the General Motors company.

But it didn't take Australians long to embrace the Holden, and it dominated the family car market until 1960, when the Ford company launched the Falcon to compete with it. Holden struck back with a model called the Kingswood and, from the late 1960s to the late 1970s, the Kingswood shared honours with the Hills Hoist as the supreme symbol of suburban life. Hundreds of thousands of Australian children were conceived in Kingswood back seats.

These days there are 10.6 million cars and trucks on Australian roads. We buy 450 000 new cars a year. The two top sellers of the mid 1990s are the Holden Commodore (with the Acclaim, a cheap family sedan, being the most popular model) and the Ford Falcon. Both are Australian-made. Third position is fought out between the Toyota Camry (Japan), the Mitsubishi Magna (Japan) and the Hyundai Excel (Korea).

But Australia's yearning for its rural mythology is apparent in another sales statistic: we are the biggest buyers of four-wheel-drive vehicles in the world. Some 4WD owners use them to bash the bush. Most use them to brave the dangers of the local shopping centre.

44
beer

*t*here was a time, back in the mid 1970s, when Australia was one of the great beer drinking nations. With an average individual consumption of 140 litres a year—that's ten cans a week for each adult—we fell behind only Germany (147 litres) and Belgium (143). But times changed fast. Now we are not even in the world's top ten. Fear of health damage and drink-driving charges, rising prices and rising wine consumption, and the ageing of the population all led to the situation in the mid 1990s where we can barely get down 96 litres each a year, and 22 litres of that is low alcohol 'lite' beer.

Brand loyalties have changed too. From the 1860s to the 1960s, the dominant drinks on the eastern seaboard were made by two Sydney families: the Tooths and the Tooheys. Your choice of amber fluid was an emblem of your religious affiliation, because the Tooheys were Irish Catholics and the Tooths were English Anglicans. Tooths

Why have you gone off light beer? I was starting to remember why I drank kept up their sales by controlling a network of pubs which were only permitted to sell their products.

But in 1976, the Trade Practices Commission ruled against 'tied' pubs, and the market opened up. Toohey's draught became the top drop and the breweries became the targets for takeovers. Tooth's was swallowed by Melbourne's Carlton and United Breweries, and Toohey's was swallowed by Alan Bond and his Perth-based Swan company. After the collapse of Bond, the New Zealand company Lion Nathan took over his beer empire, and now splits the market with CUB (which has renamed itself the Foster's Brewing Group).

The nation's most popular beers are Victoria Bitter, better known as VB (25 per cent of the market), followed by Foster's Light Ice and Carlton Gold (each about 6 per cent). Outside Australia, Foster's beer is promoted as the national drink, but in fact it appeals to less than 10 per cent of local beer buffs. Foster's is far more successful in Britain, where it has 19 per cent of the beer market—a model of colonialism in reverse.

45
lamingtons, etc

*l*amingtons—sponge cubes coated in chocolate and grated coconut—form part of a parade of foodstuffs that almost nobody eats any more but almost everybody thinks are traditional Australian fare. They seem to have been named after Baron Lamington, who was Governor of Queensland from 1895 to 1901, and started appearing in recipe books around 1909. They have a similar nostalgia value to the pavlova, a meringue covered with whipped cream and fruits, which was invented in New Zealand in the 1920s but perfected and named (after a visiting Russian ballerina) in 1935 by Bert Sachse, the chef at the Esplanade Hotel in Perth.

But if they don't really consume lamingtons any more, what do Australians actually eat for light relief? The answer is that we've stopped cooking and started shopping. A 1994 study by the research group Mintel shows the average Australian house-hold consumes 327 packs of snacks a year, at a cost of $540 (compared with $506 a year spent on fruit

and vegetables). Although our total snack consumption is behind the British, the Americans and the Irish, we beat them on biscuits, which form 28 per cent of our snack consumption (compared with 17 per cent for the Yanks). 'Australian snackers seem to be the most mature in the breadth of snack consumption,' said the Mintel report flatteringly. 'Unlike UK snackers, who show a marked preference for sweets, and US snackers, who are dominated by a desire for crisps and salty snacks, Australians are described as "menu snackers".' The typical annual snack menu includes Cherry Ripe chocolate bars, Kool Mints, Freddo frogs, Samboy Chips, Teddy Bear sweet biscuits, Cadbury Dairy Milk chocolate blocks, Ryvita crackers, Roses boxed chocs and Lifesavers.

As for kids, a survey by the Coles supermarket chain showed that their favourite lollies were the same in the mid 1990s as in the mid 1970s: 1. Snakes (gelatinous, sticky, coloured things). 2. Peppermints (mostly made by a company called Numquam for the past 80 years). 3. Barley sugars. 4. Jelly beans. 5. Party mix (also known as bowel oilers). 6. Butterscotch. 7. Raspberries. 8. Jubes. 9. Bananas. 10. Caramels. Neither raspberries nor bananas have any connection with the fruit of the same name.

46
organisations

*m*any of Australia's influential agencies are known simply by their initials. Here's a sampling:

☆ **The ABC** (Australian Broadcasting Corporation). Operating on federal government grants, it runs radio and television stations designed to provide high-quality programs for people whose needs are not met by commercial stations.

☆ **ACOSS** (Australian Council of Social Service). It's a lobby group for the poor and the handicapped.

☆ **The ACTU** (Australian Council of Trade Unions). It's a lobby group for Australia's three million union members, primarily interested in pay rates and conditions and having most influence when the Labor Party is in power.

☆ **The AMA** (Australian Medical Association). It's a lobby group for doctors, primarily

What does the ABC stand for anyway?

A Bit Commercial

Wilcox

interested in setting fees and occasionally in health issues, having most influence when the Liberal Party is in power.

☆ **ASIO** (Australian Security Intelligence Organisation). Our CIA, it spies on people and groups considered a danger to national security. Overseas spying is more likely to be done by ASIS (Australian Secret Intelligence Service) whose agents are attached to diplomatic or trade missions, or by DSD (Defence Signals Directorate) which listens in on communications from our neighbours in the south Pacific. In total, Australia employs about 2000 full-time spies.

☆ **ATSIC** (Aboriginal and Torres Strait Islander Commission). The body that represents Australia's indigenous minority.

☆ **The CSIRO** (Commonwealth Scientific and Industrial Research Organisation). Funded by the federal government to the tune of $680 million a year, its 7000 staff engage in 'application-oriented research' designed to help industry and community needs.

☆ **QANTAS** (Queensland and Northern Territory Aerial Service). Founded in 1920, it is our dominant international air carrier (two million passengers out of Australia a year) and our second domestic carrier (having slightly fewer planes than its competitor, Ansett).

☆ **The RSL** (Returned Services League). It

represents people who served in Australia's military forces, acts as a lobby group on defence (and sometimes against Asian immigration), and runs hundreds of social clubs where people can drink and play poker machines.

☆ **The RSPCA** (Royal Society for the Prevention of Cruelty to Animals). It's best known for providing pounds where Australians can leave unwanted pets, which are eventually killed if not claimed.

☆ **TELSTRA** (formerly called Telecom Australia) is a phone company two thirds owned by the Government and one third by private investors. Its main private competitor is Optus, which offers an alternative pricing system on long-distance calls. Both are supervised by AUSTEL, which must issue a permit for any phone or fax equipment, and which has decreed that by 1999, all Australian phone numbers will increase to eight digits from their previous six or seven.

47
faith

m ore Australians believe in space aliens than believe in God, despite the fact that more Australians have been to church than have been abducted by UFOs.

A 1995 survey of religious beliefs by the Saulwick research organisation found 74 per cent of adults saying they believed in God, while 20 per cent described themselves as atheists and 6 per cent as agnostics. This fits with the 1996 census, wherein 25 per cent of Australians wrote 'no religion' or left the religion section blank.

The census shows 27 per cent of Australians as Catholic, 22 per cent Anglican and 8 per cent Uniting Church. Only 3.3 per cent of the population belong to a 'non-Christian' religion, of whom Muslims and Buddhists are a third each, and Jews are 13 per cent.

But regardless of any allegiance they nominate, only 22 per cent of Australians describe themselves as regular churchgoers. The survey suggested NSW citizens are more devout (78 per cent believers and 25 per cent churchgoers) than Victorians (67 per cent and 19 per cent).

In 1995, a national survey by the Perth-based

magazine REVelation found that 80 per cent of Australians believe aliens exist somewhere in the universe, and 70 per cent believe UFOs are real. Further good news for extraterrestrials: 63 per cent of Australians believe they have the technology to visit earth, 47 per cent believe they are friendly and contact is desirable (that film *ET* has a lot to answer for), and 40 per cent believe some humans have been abducted by them. About one in ten Australians say they have had unexplained experiences that might be connected with UFOs. Spooky.

48
work

a ustralia has a workforce of nine million people, of whom 730 000 (8.1 per cent) are classified as unemployed. In the mid 1980s, the unemployment rate was six per cent and in the mid 1960s it was two per cent. But the good news between the 1980s and the 1990s was that the inflation rate dropped from 10 per cent to below three per cent. So the dole payments to the unemployed don't lose much in buying power.

The average working Australian these days earns $596 a week (compared with $455 in the mid 1980s and $80 in the mid 1960s). This statistic hides a wide variation. The nation's 3.7 million working women average $468 a week, while the 4.8 million working men average $715. But then again, men average 39 hours work a week while

women average 28 hours (not including housework, which men hardly ever do).

The retail trade is the biggest employer of Australians, who are more likely to be clerks, salespeople, or labourers than any other

108

occupation. The average earnings for sales work is $558 a week, for tradespeople is $688 and for labouring is $556. People classified as professionals average $862 a week. The chief executive of the BHP company earns $25 000 a week.

Most full-time workers in Australia are entitled to four weeks annual leave and to belong to a super-annuation scheme partly funded by their employer, who is supposed to pay a bonus three per cent of an employee's wage into a super fund. Surveys show 50 per cent of Australians say superannuation will be their main source of income after they turn 65.

49
the farm

*t*he traditional wisdom that 'Australia rides on the sheep's back' may need to be revised these days to 'Australia rides on the tourist's back'. But we're still dependent on our 147 000 farms, which cover 463 million hectares (60 per cent of the continent) and produce goods worth $27.6 billion a year.

More than 70 per cent of the wool made into the world's clothing comes from Australia's 46 000 sheep properties. In fact our 126 million sheep, most of them merinos, use half the continent as grazing land. Sadly, the world's sheep shearing record is held by a New Zealander, who managed 804 lambs in nine hours, compared with Australia's best—David Ryan, who managed 500 lambs in 7 hours 46 minutes in 1979.

With 27 million cattle, Australia is also the world's biggest exporter of beef and veal, as well as the third largest consumer of meat (each of us swallows about 70 kg of animal protein a year). We are also among the world's biggest wheat producers, with 9.7 million hectares of farmland producing around 12 million tonnes of wheat a year. In all, 391 000 Australians—only 3 per cent of the population—work in agricultural activities. That statistic is further evidence that we are the opposite of an outback culture.

50
radio

a ustralia's first public wireless broadcast happened on 23 November 1923 on Sydney radio station 2SB (soon to change its call sign to 2BL). It was a live concert of ballads and light classical music. Radio rapidly became Australia's primary information and entertainment medium, mingling news, sports, serials, quizzes, comedies and commentary. In the 1950s it made heroes out of the quizmasters Bob Dyer (who made a successful transition to television) and Jack Davey (who didn't). It launched the acting careers of Peter Finch, Rod Taylor (radio's Tarzan), John Meillon and Leonard Teale (radio's Superman).

From the 1960s, radio retreated to all-music formulas or phone-in programs in which the listeners provided their own cheap entertainment. Talkback has made a hero of the conservative commentator John Laws, heard in most States mid-morning. The highest rating commercial station in Melbourne is 3AW, and its most-phoned talk jock is Neil Mitchell. The top Sydney station is 2UE, where Alan Jones at breakfast and Stan Zemanek at night cheerfully support the Liberal Party. Government-funded ABC stations, particularly Radio National, attempt a more impartial coverage.

51
television

*h*ow do Australians spend their leisure? The latest data comes from a 'Time Use Survey' by the Australian Bureau of Statistics in 1993. It turns out that each of us devotes an hour a week to 'outdoor activity' such as bushwalking or fishing, 70 minutes a week to playing sports, 47 minutes a week to reading books and half an hour a week to watching videos. Pretty well-balanced people, wouldn't you say? Except that I left out the biggest national pastime: every Australian spends 12 hours a week watching television.

There were experimental TV transmissions here as early as 1935 in Brisbane but, for a mass audience, the first words spoken on Australian TV, on 16 September 1956, were 'Welcome to television'. The first person visible in flickering black and white on Sydney's TCN-9 was Bruce Gyngell, an announcer who went on to run the Seven network, the Broadcasting Control Board, and the Nine network. The next channel on air was Melbourne's HSV-7, on 4 November 1956, followed the next day by the first government-financed station, the ABC.

During the first year of Australian television, the programs included 'Lassie', 'Annie Oakley', 'Robin

Hood', 'Liberace', 'Father Knows Best', 'Hopalong Cassidy' and, by way of Australian content, the 'Johnny O'Connor Show'. America has continued to dominate our programming ever since. Based on ratings figures and longevity, these would be the foreign-made shows most Australians remember: 'The Saint', 'The Fugitive', 'The Dick Van Dyke Show', 'Get Smart', 'I Dream of Jeannie', 'Hawaii-50', 'The Six Million Dollar Man', 'Little House on the Prairie', 'The Rockford Files', 'The Streets of San Francisco', 'Charlie's Angels', 'Happy Days', 'MASH', and 'Disneyland'. The top Australian shows are in the next chapter.

Television changed to colour in March 1975, and we suddenly discovered that Peter Graves' hair in 'Mission Impossible' was prematurely grey, not blond.

Now we have three commercial networks, called Seven, Nine and Ten, an ABC network watched by about 15 per cent of the population, and an 'ethnic' network called SBS with arty movies and programs in languages other than English, watched by about 4 per cent of the population.

In 1995 an assortment of new 'pay TV' subscription channels began transmission by satellite, microwave and cable. They specialise in news, pop music, old movies, recent movies, old American series, business, sport and wholesome family entertainment. Australians have been slow to sign up for them, probably because we just don't have any more spare time.

52
box tops

*t*he most fondly remembered Australian-made TV shows since 1956 have been ...

☆ **A COUNTRY PRACTICE** (1981–93). A 'quality soap' which mingled realistic medical difficulties with complex emotional lives in the town of Wandin Valley.

☆ **HOMICIDE** (1966–74). Detectives in grey suits and pork-pie hats drove interminably around the Melbourne suburbs. The key figure was iron-jawed Detective McKay, played by Leonard Teale, who became an icon. 'Homicide' begat a stream of similar cop shows, including 'Division 4', 'Cop Shop' and 'Matlock Police'.

☆ **NEIGHBOURS** (1985–?). A portrait of family life in Ramsay Street, Erinsborough, a

Melbourne suburb, it launched the international careers of Kylie Minogue, Jason Donovan, and Kimberley Davies. Every weekday, 11 million British people watch 'Neighbours' and its sister soap 'Home and Away' (set in the NSW coastal town of Summer Bay) and they are so influential that linguists can now detect Australian vowel sounds in the speech of English schoolchildren. Revenge at last!

☆ **NUMBER 96** (1972–77). The first sexy soapy serial, set in a Sydney apartment block, featuring nude glimpses, frequent infidelities, and the first regular homosexual character in any Australian show.

☆ **PLAY SCHOOL** (1966–?). Every weekday morning and afternoon for three decades, this showcase for unemployed actors has cheerfully instilled moral values and practical skills in Australia's under-fives.

☆ **PRISONER** (1979–86). The lives of the inmates of a women's prison, under the iron hand of a sadistic lesbian officer named Joan 'The Freak' Ferguson.

☆ **SKIPPY** (1968–71). The tale of a very smart kangaroo, a park ranger and his family. Since roos are bad actors, there were actually 16 lookalikes playing the role.

☆ **BLUE HEELERS** (1994–?). Part soap, part crime drama, it follows the adventures of five honest cops based in the Victorian town of Mt

Thomas. Three million Australians watch it every week.

The most fondly remembered figures on Australian television have been:

☆ **BRIAN HENDERSON**. First as presenter of the pop show 'Bandstand', then as a Channel Nine newsreader, he proved the power of the nerd.

☆ **GRAHAM KENNEDY**. His larrikin wit brought him adulation and outrage on late-night variety shows from 1957 till the early 1990s. He also named Australia's award for TV excellence—the Logie (from the middle name of John Logie Baird, the inventor of television).

☆ **GARRY McDONALD**. His creation of the world's most awful interviewer and singer, Norman Gunston, in the 1970s, followed by his 1980s incarnation as the long-suffering Arthur Beare in 'Mother and Son' established him as Australia's greatest comic actor.

☆ **JANA WENDT**. Her blend of spectacular looks, incisive mind and cool manner made her our pre-eminent current-affairs presenter.

☆ **RAY MARTIN**. Australia's best-known man, because of his history as host of three top rating programs: '60 Minutes', 'The Midday Show' and 'A Current Affair'. He's the nice guy every politician wants to be interviewed by.

53
cinema

*a*ustralians now buy 70 million cinema tickets a year. This could mean that each of us goes to four movies a year, but a study by The Australian Film Commission showed that 40 per cent of Australians don't go to the pictures at all. Those who go regularly tend to be young—90 per cent of people aged 15 to 24 said they went to the flicks more than twice a year.

The most successful movies of all time in Australia (based on box office takings adjusted to modern dollar values) were:

1. The Sound of Music.
2. Gone With The Wind.
3. Crocodile Dundee.
4. Star Wars.
5. E. T.
6. Titanic
7. Babe.
8. Jaws.
9. Grease.
10. The Sting.
11. Jurassic Park.
12. The Man From Snowy River.

13. Crocodile Dundee 2.
14. Ben Hur.
15. Forrest Gump.
16. Towering Inferno.
17. Raiders of the Lost Ark.
18. Ghostbusters.
19. The Ten Commandments.
20. Independence Day.
21. Pretty Woman.
22. The Lion King.
23. Return of the Jedi.
24. Dr Zhivago.
25. Mrs Doubtfire.
26. Gallipoli.
27. My Fair Lady.
28. Alvin Purple.
29. Mad Max 2.
30. Saving Private Ryan.

Considering the general sentiment that our popular culture is dominated by Hollywood, having seven of our top 30 movies made in Australia is not a bad score.

54

our greatest movies

*a*ustralia made the world's first feature films—
Soldiers of the Cross in 1900 and *The Story
of the Kelly Gang* in 1906. We had a thriving
industry in the silent era, particularly marked by
the film version of C. J. Dennis' poem *The Sen-
timental Bloke* in 1919. An Australian animator,
Pat Sullivan, moved to New York and in 1919
created Felix the Cat, who was the world's most
successful cartoon character till Mickey Mouse
took over in the late 1920s. Australia's first epic
was *Forty Thousand Horsemen* in 1940, and in
1942 the Australian cameraman Damien Parer won
an Oscar for a documentary called *Kokoda
Frontline*.

But suddenly, after World War Two, the Australian film industry disappeared, unable to compete
with the American imports.
It was not revived until the
early 1970s, as the result of
national government financial assistance. The fad
during that decade became
historical dramas about the
origins of the Australian

Have you seen Paul Hogan's latest movie?

No, but I've read the stock market report

identity, such as *Picnic at Hanging Rock*, *Caddie*, *The Getting of Wisdom*, *Newsfront* and *My Brilliant Career*.

In the 1980s, artiness was replaced by commercialism, with the success of three *Mad Max* movies, two *Man from Snowy River* movies, and two *Crocodile Dundee*s.

In the 1990s, the prevailing style changed again. Now we go for weird comedies, preferably with lavish costumes—*Strictly Ballroom*; *The Adventures of Priscilla, Queen of the Desert*; *Muriel's Wedding*; *All Men Are Liars* and *Babe*.

Here's a shortlist of significant Australian films that are worth seeing (as opposed to *Picnic at Hanging Rock*, which is significant but slow):

☆ **CROCODILE DUNDEE** (1986). This tale of an innocent who triumphs over the evils of the big city played upon our bush mythology and turned into our most profitable international hit.

☆ **MY BRILLIANT CAREER** (1979). The first feminist costume drama introduced actor Judy Davis, who played a rebel against the conventions imposed on women.

☆ **BREAKER MORANT** (1980). This courtroom drama showed how the British sacrificed Australians for political expediency in Africa during the Boer War. It started Bryan Brown's international career.

☆ **GALLIPOLI** (1981). Another search-for-identity flick which showed how the British sacrificed Australians in Turkey during World War One.

☆ **MAD MAX** (1979), **MAD MAX TWO** (1981) and **MAD MAX THREE** (1985). Three science-fiction car-chase spectaculars in which Mel Gibson introduced his persona of the brooding loner and Australia showed it could match Hollywood for entertainment value.

☆ **THE YEAR MY VOICE BROKE** (1987) and **FLIRTING** (1991). Two gently humorous examinations of teen angst in the early 1960s, by writer–director John Duigan, which ring true in the memories of many Australians.

☆ **STRICTLY BALLROOM** (1993). A flamboyant hit about youthful imagination triumphing over conservatism, it showed that Australian moviemaking couldn't be typecast. Its successful silliness opened the door for *Muriel*, *Priscilla* and *Babe*.

☆ **SHINE** (1996). A romanticised biography of the mentally ill pianist David Helfgott, it made $130 million around the world and won a Best Actor Oscar for Geoffrey Rush.

☆ **THE CASTLE** (1997). This tale of a Suburban family battling to save their home from an airport expansion is a celebration of ordinariness.

55
direct from Hollywood

*a*ustralian film directors have a habit of moving overseas and finding so much success that they rarely return. This traitorous band includes . . .

☆ **GILLIAN ARMSTRONG**, who started her brilliant career with *My Brilliant Career* in 1979 and has shuttled between here and America ever since, making *Mrs Soffel* in 1984 and *Little Women* in 1994.

☆ **BRUCE BERESFORD**, who got laughs with *The Adventures of Barry McKenzie* in 1972, then respect with *Breaker Morant* in 1980. His move to Hollywood led him to the Oscar-winning *Driving Miss Daisy*.

☆ **JANE CAMPION**, who was born in New Zealand but claimed by Australia because she studied at the Australian Film and Television School and filmed *Sweetie* here in 1989. Then she had the nerve to establish her international reputation with two films set in New Zealand—*Angel At My Table* and *The Piano*.

☆ **GEORGE MILLER**, who proved himself a master of action with *Mad Max* in 1979 and a clever comic organiser with *The Witches of*

Eastwick in 1987. He returned to Australia in 1995 to make a pig talk in *Babe*.

☆ **PHIL NOYCE**, who made his name here in 1978 with the 1950s nostalgia tale *Newsfront* and now directs action spectaculars such as *Patriot Games* in Hollywood.

☆ **FRED SCHEPISI**, who showed his seriousness with *The Devil's Playground* (1976) and *The Chant of Jimmie Blacksmith* (1978), then his lightness of touch with the American hit *Roxanne* (1986). He returned in 1987 to make *Evil Angels* (called *A Cry in the Dark* in America), the story of the Azaria Chamberlain case (see Chapter 29 'what puzzles us').

☆ **PETER WEIR**, who proved that movies could be art with *Picnic at Hanging Rock* (1975) and *Gallipoli* (1981), then mastered the art of entertainment with *Witness* and *The Truman Show*.

☆ **BAZ LUHRMANN**, who showed a flair for the campy in *Strictly Ballroom* and went on to direct the highly profitable *Romeo and Juliet* as a modern gang warfare spectacular.

☆ **P. J. HOGAN**, who directed *Muriel's Wedding* then, sticking with his speciality, made *My Best Friend's Wedding* in Hollywood with Julia Roberts.

☆ **JOHN SEALE**, who is not (yet) a director but as camera operator won the 1996 Best Cinematography Oscar for *The English Patient*.

56
videos

a ustralians are video freaks. We own the most VCRs per capita of any nation (they're in 87 per cent of Australia's TV-owning homes, compared with 84 per cent in America and Britain) and we rent 220 million videos a year. The taste of our video-renters differs somewhat from that of our cinemagoers. We're suckers for crime thrillers, romantic comedies and special effects spectaculars.

What we don't like is sex. As measured by *Video Trader* magazine's surveys of stores, here are the most rented movies of the mid 90s ... In 1994: *The Firm, Cliffhanger, A Few Good Men*, and *The Fugitive*. In 1995: *Speed, Pulp Fiction, Forrest Gump*, and *The Mask*. In 1996: *Braveheart, Seven, Jumanji, While You Were Sleeping*, and *GoldenEye*. The nearest any came to nudity was when Mel Gibson bared his bum in *Braveheart*.

Our favourite stars, judged by frequency in the rentals lists, are Sandra Bullock, Tom Hanks, Sylvester Stallone, John Travolta, Meg Ryan, Robin Williams, Tom Cruise, Demi Moore and Jim Carrey.

When it comes to buying rather than renting, kids rule the decision making. Our top selling videos of all time are *The Lion King, Titanic, Toy Story, Aladdin, Babe* and *Star Wars*.

57
sports

*W*e are a nation of sports fanatics. Not that most of us play sport, of course, but we like to watch, preferably on TV. An event such as a State of Origin rugby league match can attract a television audience of more than three million people, even including states that don't play rugby league. This phenomenon of watching, but not doing, drove the federal government in the 1970s to fund a TV advertising campaign with the slogan 'Life. Be In It.' in which a couch potato named Norm boasted of being a 'well-rounded sportsman'. It was successful in making Norm a recognisable symbol of the Aussie male. To the extent that we play games, the most popular are golf and tennis.

I'll deal with football and cricket in the next chapters, but in other sports, the legends to know are:

☆ **JOHN BERTRAND,** who skippered a yacht called *Australia II* to win the America's Cup in 1983, the first time it had ever been out of America's hands.

Dad, can I wear your "Life Be In It" t-shirt?

Yeah. It doesn't fit me any more

☆ **JACK BRABHAM,** who was world champion racing driver three times, the last time in 1966 in a car he designed and built himself.

☆ **KAY COTTEE,** who in 1988 became the first woman to sail solo and unassisted round the world.

☆ **MARGARET COURT,** who, between 1960 and 1973, won more major tennis titles than any player, male or female, including three Wimbledon, five US and four French singles titles.

☆ **HERB ELLIOTT,** the world's greatest one mile and 1500 metre runner, who broke the four-minute mile 17 times and won a gold medal at the 1960 Olympics for running 1500 metres in 3 minutes 35.6 seconds.

☆ **DAWN FRASER,** who set 27 individual swimming records, and won gold medals in three Olympics for the 100 metres freestyle. She was banned from competitive swimming in 1965 by the Australian Swimming Union for supposedly disobeying orders of team managers.

☆ **ANDREW GAZE,** a local legend in basketball, a sport where young Australians usually admire black Americans. Playing for the Melbourne Tigers, he holds the record of 9161 points in 283 games between 1984 and 1995, averaging 32.3 points per game.

☆ **EVONNE GOOLAGONG** (married name

Cawley), the first Aboriginal tennis champion and the first mother to win Wimbledon (in 1971, defeating her hero Margaret Court). She won the Australian Open four times in the 1970s and Wimbledon again in 1980.

☆ **ROD LAVER**, who won the tennis 'grand slam' (the French, US, Australian and Wimbledon singles titles) in 1962 and in 1969.

☆ **WALTER LINDRUM**, the world's greatest billiards player, who held 57 world records when he retired in 1950, and in 1932 set a record score of 4137 in 2 hours 55 minutes.

☆ **HEATHER McKAY**, the world's greatest squash player, who won every Australian women's title from 1960 to 1973, and 16 British Opens. She lost only two matches in a 20-year career.

☆ **HUBERT OPPERMAN**, the world's greatest cyclist, who set a still-unbroken record of 1384.4 kilometres in 24 hours in 1932. Then he went into politics and became Minister for Immigration in 1963.

☆ **LIONEL ROSE**, who became the first Aboriginal boxing champion when he took the world bantamweight title in 1968, and successfully defended it twice in 1969.

☆ **PETER THOMSON**, who was the first Australian to win the British Open Golf championship (in 1954 and four more times).

58
football

*t*he single greatest preoccupation of Australian males is football. But they confuse themselves by following four different codes, with audiences varying according to regional and ethnic differences. In order of popularity, they are:

☆ **RUGBY LEAGUE.** It's a game played mainly in New South Wales, Queensland, and Canberra, and began in 1907 as a breakaway from the prevailing Rugby Union. The emphasis is on brawn. Nowadays the lure of big money has divided it into two competitions—ten teams of Super League (players who signed up with Rupert Murdoch) and 12 teams of ARL (players who stuck with the traditional clubs). Australia's international team, the Kangaroos, usually wins against the French and the New Zealanders, and is roughly even with

The difference between Rugby

... and AFL

Wilcox

the British. The League's legends include: Wally Lewis, who captained Queensland and Australia in the 1980s and played in more winning Australian Test teams than any other player; Mal Meninga, a super goal kicker who scored a record 254 points in 40 Tests between 1982 and 1993, and captained the Canberra Raiders in four Grand Finals and the Kangaroos in 12 tests; Dally Messenger, known as 'the Master', who set a goal kicking record of 82 metres in 1909.

☆ **AUSTRALIAN RULES**. Invented in the 1850s to keep Australian cricketers fit during the winter, it became the dominant code in Victoria, South Australia, Western Australia and Tasmania. It is the most interesting form of football to watch because the players engage in graceful leaps. In Melbourne, it draws fanatical adherents equally from all classes, while Rugby League is a more working-class game. Grand Finals in late September attract TV audiences of two million. The legends of AFL (Australian Football League) include: Haydn Bunton, who played for Melbourne's Fitzroy club and then for Perth's Subiaco club in the 1930s and 40s, and won six 'best and fairest player' medals; Roy Cazaly, a player for the South Melbourne club in the 1930s who could jump 1.5 metres, and who inspired the rallying cry 'Up there, Cazaly'.

☆ **RUGBY UNION**. First played by soldiers at the Sydney barracks in 1829, based on a game developed at the English school called Rugby six years earlier, it became the dominant winter game of the Australian colonies until 1907, when players seeking better payment split off and formed the Rugby League. Rugby Union never recovered. The competition is now mainly between NSW and Queensland, and internationally against various British teams and New Zealand, South Africa, France and Fiji. The legends of the Union include: Mark Ella, a record-breaking try scorer who became the first Aboriginal player to captain an Australian football team, and whose brothers Glen and Garry were almost as skilful; Nick Farr-Jones, who captained the Australian team in its most successful period between 1988 and 1991.

☆ **SOCCER**. First played here in 1880, it has never attracted enough adherents to allow the creation of a world-class team. Soccer is now followed mainly by Australians of European or South American origin. The dominant teams are South Melbourne, Adelaide City, the Brisbane Strikers and such Sydney teams as Marconi, APIA and Olympic. Australian soccer's finest moment came in 1973 when the Socceroos played in the World Cup Finals in Munich. They didn't win a match.

59
cricket

*t*he first recorded cricket match in Australia happened in 1803, on a patch of grass which is now in Sydney's Hyde Park, between officers of the supply ship *Calcutta* and some free settlers, but no convicts or Aborigines. Cricket became the dominant summer sport of the colony. In 1862 the first visiting English team played 13 matches in Sydney and Melbourne, winning 11. In 1868 the first Australian team visited England—13 Aboriginal players who also gave demonstrations of boomerang throwing. They won 14 matches, lost 14 and drew 19.

And so began the great tradition of rivalry between Britain and Australia, played out each year in Test matches for a prize called The Ashes—a wooden cup filled with the ashes of a burnt stump and some balls. The symbolism originated in 1882 when Australia first defeated England and the *Sporting Times* wrote that English cricket should be cremated and the ashes sent to Australia. These days Australia also plays Tests against the West Indies, South Africa, India, Pakistan and New Zealand. Over history, we have more victories than losses with all those teams, so we can reasonably claim to be the greatest cricketing nation in the world.

Within Australia, matches between states are played for a prize called the Sheffield Shield, donated in 1892 by England's Earl of Sheffield. New South Wales has held the shield most often, while Queensland became famous as the perennial loser, earning the slogan: 'Queensland—beautiful one day, out for 75 runs the next'. In 1995 Queensland astonished the nation by winning the Sheffield Shield for the first time.

The legends of cricket include:

☆ **ALAN BORDER,** a batsman who holds the record for making the most runs in a Test career—10 695 from 147 appearances between 1978 and 1994, with 85 of them as Australia's captain.

☆ **GREG CHAPPELL,** a batsman who made 7110 runs in 88 matches between 1966 and 1984, but who embarrassed Australia as captain in 1981 by ordering his brother Trevor to bowl underarm on the last ball to prevent New Zealand hitting any more runs.

☆ **DENNIS LILLEE,** a bowler who holds the record of taking 355 wickets in 70 Test matches (between 1971 and 1984).

☆ **MARK 'TUBBY' TAYLOR,** who retired as Australia's captain in 1999, aged 34, after batting 7525 runs in 104 Tests and equalling Bradman's best score of 334 runs in a single match.

60
Don Bradman

a bout the most blasphemous thing you could ever say to an Australian is 'But he was only a cricketer', if the conversation should turn to Don Bradman. Whenever people are asked to name the greatest living Australian, Bradman tops the polls. It's mysterious, because most Australians now living have never seen him play (he retired from active cricket in 1948).

Bradman grew up in Bowral, NSW and scored his first centuries for the local cricket team in 1920, at the age of 12. He represented Australia in 52 international Test matches, averaging 99.9 runs each time he batted (when for other players, an average of 50 is considered pretty good). He so demoralised the English players that in 1932 they developed a brutal bowling technique called 'body-line' that involved trying to get the ball to hit the batsman's head or body.

In Bradman's final Test innings in 1948, before a frenzied crowd, he needed only four runs to bring his average up to 100. But he was bowled out for a duck (zero runs). Australians know the explanation: he couldn't see for the tears in his eyes.

61
the Olympics

*a*ustralia is one of only five countries in the world to have participated in every Olympic Games since they were revived in 1896. There's a fair chance we'll be participating in the Olympics in the year 2000 as well, because they will be held in Sydney. We should expect to do well, too, because out of the past 24 Olympics, we won the second highest total of medals (35, including 13 gold) in 1956, when they were held in Melbourne.

Our most pathetic performance in recent years was at the 1976 Olympics in Montreal, when we won no gold medals and only one silver. This produced a mass outbreak of soul-searching for a nation which had long regarded itself as a land of champions. The federal government set up an Institute of Sport in Canberra as a place to train

potential Olympians not only in fitness but in motivation and, by the 1984 games in Los Angeles, we were back to winning four gold and eight silver medals.

Our greatest Olympic

athletes have been the swimmers Murray Rose and Dawn Fraser, who each won four gold medals in the 1950s and 60s, and the runner Betty Cuthbert, who won three gold medals in 1956 and another in 1964.

Australia's best performance ever was in Atlanta in 1996, where we won 41 medals, 13 of them gold, and came seventh out of 187 countries. The most watched athletes were Kieren Perkins, who won gold in the men's 1500 metres freestyle swimming, and Cathy Freeman, the Aboriginal runner who won silver in the women's 400 metre race. Australians were less united in their enthusiasm for our display at the closing ceremony, which included giant rubber kangaroos wobbling on the backs of pushbikes ridden by a group of schoolchildren.

The year 2000 Olympics will be mainly staged at a series of venues in the Sydney suburb of Homebush. Australians have been watching with increasing scepticism as early promises to create a 'green games' have been diluted, the projected costs have soared, various officials have been accused of giving or receiving luxurious treatment in return for votes on the international Olympic controlling body, and the organisers have revealed that Australians will have to enter a lottery for the few tickets left for locals. But we retain the expectation that the Olympics will create a tourist bonanza, and we are building hotels accordingly.

62
Gough Whitlam

*t*he most interesting politician in Australian history is Gough Whitlam, a symbol of how an idealist can be both visionary and blind. He was a middle-class lawyer who joined the Labor Party in the 1950s when it was dominated by narrow-minded union officials, and transformed the party from within. By 1972, when Whitlam led the party to its first election victory in 23 years with the slogan 'It's Time', Labor had reformist policies on the environment, education, health, social welfare and redistribution of wealth.

In office for three years, the Whitlam Government withdrew Australian troops from the Vietnam War and ended conscription, removed the last vestiges of the White Australia Policy, abolished university fees, increased funding to the neediest schools and began a national health insurance scheme. But Whitlam's blind spot was economics and, by 1975, with inflation and unemployment rising, some of his ministers were involved in risky attempts to borrow money overseas.

The Opposition parties, led by Malcolm Fraser, had a majority in the Senate, one of the two houses of the Australian parliament, and refused to pass the government's budget bills. The Governor-General, John Kerr, dismissed Whitlam and ordered an election of both houses, in which Labor was defeated, despite such slogans as 'Shame, Fraser, Shame' and 'Maintain the rage'. Whitlam stayed on as Labor leader but lost another election in 1977. He retired from parliament and now applies his considerable wit and intellect to polishing his image as an elder statesman.

63
Robert Menzies

*t*he second most interesting Australian politician is Robert Menzies, who is remembered not so much for any particular thing he did (though he formed the Liberal Party and involved Australia in the Vietnam War) but as the symbol of an era.

He was Prime Minister of Australia from 1949 to his retirement in 1966, a period of economic growth and security. Conservatives visualise the Menzies years as a golden age when women respected their menfolk and stayed home to look after the kids, when the government maintained eternal vigilance against communism, when Australians were white people of English background and Aborigines stayed out of sight, and foreigners were allowed in only to do jobs beneath the dignity of Australians.

Menzies was a devoted Anglophile, famous for quoting this piece of poetry to the Queen of England: 'I did but see her passing by, and yet I love her till I die'. But, in 1965, he happily joined with the United States government in committing troops to 'fight communism' in Vietnam, and introduced conscription of 20-year-old Australian men to ensure there were enough bodies.

Since then, the Liberal Party has never found a leader up to his standard. The search continues as the legend grows.

64
taxes

*a*ustralians pay about 160 billion dollars a year in taxes to State and Federal governments, of which about $66 billion is personal income tax. The personal tax rate is 20 cents in the dollar if you earn around $20 000 a year, rising to 47 cents in the dollar above $50 000. The company tax rate is 36 cents in the dollar.

What do we get for our money? The governments spend about $29 billion a year on health, $25 billion on education, $52 billion on social security and welfare, $8 billion on what they call 'public order and safety' (police and courts) and $9 billion on defence. It doesn't seem too bad a deal.

Some people have found ways of avoiding paying their taxes, presumably not intending to use hospitals, schools, roads or police protection. A report issued in 1995 by the Taxation Office noted that in the latest year studied, no tax was paid by 44 per cent of people running video hire shops, 37 per cent of supermarket owners, 42 per cent of fruit and vegetable store

How did you get to be so rich?

Spent a million on tax avoidance and deducted it as an overhead owners and 41 per cent of owners of fast food shops. The office found that 500 lawyers—about 10 per cent of the profession—paid no tax despite having an average business income of $125 000 each. Nearly 1000 acountants paid no tax despite earning $42 million between them. And 300 dentists paid no tax despite averaging gross earnings of $146 266.

You might feel sorry for these people, whose expenses are so high they actually make no taxable income. Or you might feel that in future you need have no qualms about biting your dentist's finger, suing your lawyer, stealing your accountant's biro and failing to rewind your rented videos.

During 1999, the Federal Government planned to introduce a 10 per cent Goods and Services Tax (GST) on everything sold. The theory was that this would allow a reduction in income taxes and let the tax office collect money from people who had previously found ways of avoiding tax on their earnings.

65
crime

*W*hen it comes to violence, Australia is one of the world's safest nations, with a murder rate of 2 per 100 000 (compared with the US rate of 8, the Swiss rate of 4 and the British rate of 1). Our most popular crime is 'unlawful entry with intent'—417 845 of these are recorded by police each year. Next comes car theft (130 406), and assault (123 940). Western Australia has the highest rate of burglary and car theft, while Queensland is tops for assault and attempted murder. It must be the heat.

And how many of us are still convicts? There are 19 100 people currently in jail in Australia, about 95 per cent of them males. Around 14 per cent are in for breaking and entering, 13 per cent for sex offences, 10 per cent for drug dealing and 9 per cent for homicide. Recent revelations about police corruption, particularly in Sydney, have made some Australians wonder how any criminals end up in jail at all.

66
games of chance

*i*t's been said that Australians would bet on two flies crawling up a wall and, indeed, we spend more per head on gambling activities (each of us blows $2 500 a year) than any nation in the western world. But the real gambling addicts in this country are the State governments, which have become dependent on revenues from poker machines, lotteries, racing and casinos. State governments (except Western Australia, which has restricted gambling because of the social damage) earn $3.4 billion a year in taxes from the gambling industry. They say the industry has created 32 000 jobs, and without the revenue, governments would have to make voters pay higher taxes.

We spend most of our gambling money on what Americans call 'slot machines' and we call 'the

The Punters' Code

I reckon, if it ain't fixed...

...Don't back it

Wilcox

pokies'. There are 120 000 of these one-armed bandits in Australia, and we put $25 billion through them every year (and win back $21 billion). Next comes horse and dog racing, on which we spend $9.3 billion (and win back $7.9 billion), followed by lotteries (including Lotto, keno, football pools and instant money games) on which we spend $3.4 billion and win back $2.1 billion.

Consider those figures another way—on average, every Australian loses $214 a year on the pokies, $74 a year on racing, and $74 a year on lotteries.

All this is before we've considered the glamorous casinos which have sprung up in every capital city. There are 14 of them, and they make $2 billion a year from their gaming tables and machines. But I forgot: the casinos are designed to extract money from foreign tourists. Australians are much too sensible to spend their time and money like that. You can bet on it.

67
the Melbourne Cup

a horse race called the Melbourne Cup holds the attention of most Australians at 3.20 p.m. on the first Tuesday of every November. In fact, it's Melbourne's only claim to fame—as far as non-Victorian Australians are concerned.

The preferred method of betting on the Cup is the office sweep, whereby everyone puts in five dollars and the horses are allocated at random to the contestants, with the entire pot divided amongst the winner and the two placegetters. This eliminates the need to know anything about the horses while requiring that time be taken off work to watch the race.

The first Melbourne Cup was run in 1861 and the winner was a horse named Archer (who won again in 1862). It used to be a two mile race, which made it last long enough to be suspenseful, but the suspense was reduced a bit in 1972 when the metric system came in, and the distance was shortened by 18 metres to 3200 metres.

The most amazing winner of the Melbourne Cup was Carbine, who carried a record weight of 66 kilograms and managed the distance in a record time of 3 minutes 28.25 seconds. That was in 1890. But Carbine never became a legend. He was overshadowed by the horse on the next page.

68
Phar Lap

*t*he most loved horse in Australian folklore is a large and ungainly chestnut gelding called Phar Lap, nicknamed 'The Red Terror'. He was born in New Zealand and died in America, but Australians claim him because he fits our self-image as a nation of battlers, and because he provides a reason to hold a grudge against the Yanks. He's the only horse to be the hero of an Australian movie.

Phar Lap kept triumphing against adversity to win 37 of his 51 races, including the Melbourne Cup in 1930. He was ready to beat every horse in America when he was taken there in 1932 but, after winning only one race in Mexico, he was found dead in his stall.

The usual theory is that the perpetrators were jealous Americans. In 1936, Phar Lap's trainer Tommy Woodcock (a legend by association) said he suspected a Californian gangster nicknamed 'The Brazilian' of poisoning the horse with arsenic. Another theory was that the Red Terror's part-owner, an

Phar Lap's Death:
The Grassy Knoll Theory

Hey— look at that grassy knoll

American named David Davis, had poisoned him as part of a (never explained) conspiracy with race-fixers.

Tommy Woodcock died in 1985, after which it was reported that he had made a deathbed confession: all his life he had been racked with guilt that he may have killed Phar Lap by accidentally over-dosing him with an arsenic-based tonic. But we don't talk much about that theory.

Phar Lap's huge heart, regarded as a national icon, is preserved in formalin waiting to be displayed in the yet-to-be-built National Museum of Australia. His skeleton is in the National Museum of New Zealand in Wellington, and his stuffed skin is in the Museum of Victoria in Melbourne.

69
our clothes

C asual is the word for the way Australians dress. No observer watching crowds in the middle of Perth or Sydney is going to mistake those cities for Paris, although Melbourne people like to think they have more elegance than the other capitals. Our fashion breakthroughs have been of a peculiar kind, as this sampling may indicate . . .

☆ **BERLEI BRAS**. A Melbourne corset-maker named Fred R. Burley commissioned Sydney University scientists in 1927 to study the shape of Australian women. After measuring 6000 of them, they concluded there were five basic figure types, and Berlei undergarments were moulded accordingly. Mr Burley thought his name needed a little change to become suitable for ladies' intimates, and Australian women have trusted Berlei ever since.

☆ **THE BIKINI**. It was invented by a Frenchman in 1946 and named after the place where America tested its

Dress-down day in the Building Industry

Mon-Thurs   Friday

atom bomb, but it was pioneered here. In late 1946 a Miss Pat Riley was ordered by police to leave Bondi beach for wearing a two-piece swimming costume made of blue netting—a battle that was to recur until the final test case at Bondi in 1961, when an actress was fined three pounds for the same offence. These days only the bottom halves of bikinis get much use at Bondi.

☆ **BLUNDSTONES**. Invented in the 1870s in Tasmania, and still made there, these rural work boots are now the hippest urban footwear of Britain and Europe, transcending even Doc Martens.

☆ **SPEEDOS**. The 'Aussie cossie' was first made in 1929 by MacRae Knitting Mills of Sydney, which later renamed itself Speedo. By the 1970s, Speedo had become the official supplier to all 52 swimming countries in both the Munich and Montreal Olympics. The fashion has now moved from sleek to saggy, as board shorts outnumber racing togs on many Australian beaches, but for those who want to move fast in the water, there's only one choice.

☆ **STUBBIES**. Two vital Australian symbols go by this name: a squat beer bottle and a squat pair of shorts. The shorts were created by a Brisbane company in 1972 and have since sold more than 40 million pairs, though they are now in decline. These days they are owned by the American cake company Sara Lee. In navy blue, with singlet and work boots, Stubbies were the uniform of labouring men and, with T-shirt and thongs, they were the uniform of the suburban weekend.

☆ **THONGS**. The rubber sandals with the strip between the toes are called jandals or flip-flops in the rest of the world, but we made them our own as the perfect companion to Stubbies (of both types) and the perfect protection against broken glass at beach or barbie.

☆ **UGG BOOTS**. Made from merino sheepskins, this warm and comfy footwear is regarded as daggy in Australia and the height of grunge fashion in California, where they are marketed as 'surf boots'. About $30 million worth of Uggs are sold in America each year, and Americans are now the majority shareholders in Ugg Holdings.

☆ **R. M. WILLIAMS**. In the 1930s, Reginald Murray Williams started making and selling durable clothes for bush battlers. Now his company is owned by two media entrepreneurs, Kerry Stokes of the Seven TV Network and Ken Cowley of News Limited, and his moleskin trousers, elastic-sided riding boots, hats and overcoats are fashionable and profitable exports to Britain, New Zealand, Dubai and Japan. Williams himself, now in his 80s, concentrates on running the Stockman's Hall of Fame in Longreach, Queensland.

70
our writers

a shortlist of Australia's most important authors would have to include:

☆ **PETER CAREY**, an advertising agent who started writing fantasy stories in the 1970s, and then produced two definitive novels about Australia—*Illywhacker* and *Oscar and Lucinda*. He now lives in New York.

☆ **MANNING CLARK**, our best-known historian, whose six-volume *A History of Australia* interpreted the white settlement of Australia with sympathy for the underdog. He died in 1991.

☆ **BRYCE COURTENAY**, a South African-born former advertising executive whose first novel, *The Power of One*, sold four million copies worldwide and was filmed. Next he wrote an account of his son's death from AIDS, called *April Fool's Day* and in late 1995 released a 'shamelessly commercial' novel called *The Potato Factory*, the first part of an Australian historical trilogy.

☆ **HELEN GARNER**, whose novel *Monkey Grip* portrayed a life of sex, drugs and rock and roll in the inner city in the 1970s, and whose long essay *The First Stone* challenged concepts of sexual harassment in the 1990s.

☆ **THOMAS KENEALLY,** who specialises in novels about oppression—convicts in *Bring Larks and Heroes*, Aborigines in *The Chant of Jimmie Blacksmith* and Jews in *Schindler's Ark* (which became the Oscar-winning film *Schindler's List*).

☆ **HENRY LAWSON,** who was the first purveyor in literature of what became our prevailing myths about mateship, sacrifice, larrikinism and tall poppy cutting. He also made the first passionate case for Australia to become a republic. His best short stories were collected as *Joe Wilson and his Mates* in 1901 and he was the first Australian writer to be given a state funeral (in 1922).

☆ **DAVID MALOUF,** a former English lecturer whose first novel, *Johnno*, about a Brisbane boyhood, was published in 1975. His most ambitious novel is *The Great World*,

which examines the relationship between official history and personal history.

☆ **COLLEEN McCULLOUGH,** our most commercially successful novelist in the

American market, notably with *The Thorn Birds*, who now lives on Norfolk Island and regularly turns out potboilers.

☆ **RUTH PARK**, who grew up in New Zealand but portrayed Australia's inner-city poverty in *The Harp in the South* and *Poor Man's Orange* in the 1940s and went on to charm children with *The Muddle-Headed Wombat* and *Playing Beattie Bow*.

☆ **PATRICK WHITE**, who won the Nobel Prize for literature in 1973 and died in 1990. David Marr's gossipy biography of White makes livelier reading than any of White's novels, but if you want to challenge yourself, try *Voss*, about a mad explorer crossing the desert, or *The Eye of the Storm* about an individual's triumph over hardship.

☆ **DAVID WILLIAMSON**, our most successful playwright, who produces a social satire every year (notably *The Removalists*, *Don's Party* and *Emerald City*) as well as frequent filmscripts (notably *Gallipoli* and *Phar Lap*).

☆ **TIM WINTON**, who has written fifteen books, usually about poignant family relationships, and twice won the Miles Franklin literary award. He is best known for *Cloudstreet* and *That Eye, The Sky* which was filmed, and in 1995 he was shortlisted for Britain's Booker prize for a novel set in Europe called *The Riders*.

71
our biggest books

*a*ustralians are prolific readers. Our favourite literature is autobiographies, particularly of local people who reinforce our image of ourselves as cheerful battlers against adversity. The most significant books by and about Australians include . . .

☆ **THE FATAL SHORE**, the first history of convict life to capture the imagination of Australians who found our history boring at school. Written in 1986 by the New York-based art critic Robert Hughes.

☆ **A FORTUNATE LIFE**, the autobiography of Albert Facey, who started work on outback properties in Western Australia at the age of eight, served at Gallipoli, and worked as a tram driver while teaching himself to read and write. It was published in 1981 and Facey died the following year, aged 88. It has sold 600 000 copies.

☆ **FROM STRENGTH TO STRENGTH**, the autobiography of Sara Henderson, who endured emotional and physical hardship on an outback cattle property with a philandering husband. Published in 1992, it has sold 400 000 copies, and her sequel, *The*

Strength In Us All, has sold 300 000.

✩ **THE MAGIC PUDDING,** a 1918 comic novel for adults and kids, written and illustrated by Norman Lindsay. Its rough and jolly characters included a koala called Bunyip Bluegum and an argumentative pudding named Albert, who grew back whenever you had a slice of him.

✩ **MY BRILLIANT CAREER,** a 1901 novel by Miles Franklin about a rural woman who refuses to accept the inevitability of marriage.

✩ **MY PLACE,** the autobiography of Sally Morgan, who learned in adult life that she was a Western Australian Aboriginal and not an Indian as she had been told, and who discovered the hardships her mother and grandmother had endured. Published in 1987, it has sold 400 000 copies.

✩ **REINVENTING AUSTRALIA,** an analysis by social anthropologist Hugh Mackay, published in 1993, of the rise of anxiety in our society as the result of revolutions in gender roles, work roles and moral values.

✩ **TALES OF SNUGGLEPOT AND CUDDLEPIE,** the first children's book to use native animals and plants instead of the English imagery which had puzzled generations of Australian children. It was written and illustrated in 1918 by May Gibbs. Now no Australian can pass a banksia bush without fear of attack by the Big Bad Banksia Men.

✩ **THE HAND THAT SIGNED THE PAPER** was supposedly a novel about a Ukrainian war criminal, based on the family history of a young author named Helen Demidenko. It was attacked as anti-semitic on its release, and parts were alleged to have been plagiarised, but it won the Miles Franklin literary award in 1995. Then its author turned out to be Helen Darville, the daughter of an English immigrant family, who had faked her Ukrainian background.

The Australia Council, which administers federal government aid to artists and writers, did a survey in 1995 which revealed that 55 per cent of women and 42 per cent of men say they are regular readers of books—a decline from 57 per cent and 48 per cent in 1989. Adult fiction accounts for 36 per cent of books read, followed by children's books (15 per cent) and self-help (12 per cent). Among people who had read a book in the past week, 29 per cent said it was by an Australian.

Books which sold more than 100 000 copies in Australia during the 1990s included *The Celestine Prophecy* by James Redfield, *Men Are From Mars, Women Are From Venus* by John Gray, *The Shipping News* by E. Annie Proulx, *The Penguin Book of Australian Jokes* by Phillip Adams and Patrice Newell, *The Liver Cleansing Diet* by Sandra Cabot, *The Horse Whisperer* by Nicholas Evans, *The Runaway Jury* by John Grisham, and *The Green Mile* by Stephen King. As well, we buy six million copies a year of the romance novels published by Harlequin, MIRA Books, Silhouette and Mills and Boon.

72
Dad and Dave

*a*ustralia's fictitious view of itself as a land of bush battlers is reinforced by two characters who have been immortalised in stories, novels, plays, radio and television series, films and jokes. They are Dad and Dave, a couple of farming yokels from a region called Snake Gully, who get regularly conned by the city slickers but never lose their innocence.

They were created by a Brisbane clerk named Arthur Hoey Davis, who wrote under the name Steele Rudd for the *Bulletin* magazine during the 1890s. His stories were first collected in a book called *On Our Selection* in 1899. Dad's wife (played by Joan Sutherland in the latest film) is known simply as Mum, while Dave's girlfriend, usually the smartest of the characters, is Mabel.

A typical joke: Dave learns from his doctor that he has less than 24 hours to live, so he goes home that night, tells Mabel the bad news, and says that they had better make love. They do so, and fall asleep. An hour later, Dave wakes Mabel and they make love again. An hour later, when Dave shakes Mabel awake, she says: 'Aw, Dave, it's all right for you, but I've got to get up in the morning.'

An example of how Dad and Dave have come to symbolise 'old Australian' (ie Anglo-Saxon) values appeared in a 1995 interview with the Liberal Party leader, John Howard, in which he apologised for his apparent reluctance to accept the multicultural face of modern Australia. 'I guess the trick is to keep the good bits of Dad and Dave and add on other good bits,' he said. 'To embrace the tolerance and sophistication that postwar immigration has given us does not require us to jettison the inherent values of the Dad and Dave stereotype. It's possible to blend them together into a better product.'

73
the way we eat

a short history of Australian food, or the race from roasts to ravioli ...

Australian food was almost ruined by the English and the Irish, but at the last minute it was saved by the Chinese, the Italians, the Vietnamese and the Thais.

For the first 50 000 years of human habitation on this continent, humans ate sparsely but well. The Aborigines developed eating patterns in harmony with the vast variety of locally available plants, animals and seafood. They dried and carried round with them fruits such as the quandong and the kakadu plum which have up to 50 times the vitamin C content of oranges. When the English arrived, they ignored all these local resources and lived on imported rations, gradually supplemented by European crops and animals that could be culti-vated here. Good eating meant lots of beef or mutton, washed down with tea or rum.

By the late 19th century, some of the Chinese who

158

came for the Gold Rush of the 1850s started opening cafes in the suburbs and the country towns and, by the early 20th century, exotic eating meant sweet and sour pork, chicken and almonds, and beef with black bean sauce. At home, most Australians ate tinned tomato soup, grilled steak with frozen peas and, for dessert, tinned pineapple and ice cream. On Sundays, they ate roast leg of lamb and potatoes.

It was not until mass migration from Europe in the 1950s that real changes began. Italian and Greek immigrants realised they had landed in a culinary wasteland and set about growing vegetables and opening restaurants. The eating-out specials became spaghetti bolognese, scaloppine with mushrooms, and lemon gelato. In 1954, the first eggplant went on sale in Australia.

But in the late 1960s, a time of wealth and social experimentation, our interest in food grew rapidly. The Italian invasion was followed by the French revolution. French cafes started to appear on every suburban corner, often run by Australian amateurs working from Paris cookbooks. The formula restaurant meal became quiche Lorraine, duck a l'orange, and creme caramel. By the late 1970s, Australia's urban foodies had turned this into nouvelle cuisine, and our chefs found that nothing succeeded like excess. Kiwi fruit and tamarillo decorated every plate. Game birds were stuffed with shrimp mousse, seated on beds of cream and cucumber, and covered with passionfruit sauce.

The late 1970s also saw an influx of Vietnamese refugees who introduced Australians to a new range of delicate taste sensations at bargain prices. The Vietnamese fad was soon replaced by Thai, with its jolts of salt, chilli and sugar, and, throughout the 1980s, small Thai restaurants materialised in the suburbs as rapidly as French restaurants did in the early 1970s. The standard restaurant meal became fishcakes, satay pork and mixed noodles.

In the 1990s, all the formulas have merged into something called 'Modern Australian' cooking. In the bistros of our inner cities, char-grilled tuna lies on a bed of baba ganoush; poached chicken breast nestles into couscous and chilli jam; barbecued octopus is wrapped in radicchio and scattered with handfuls of coriander; baby pizzas are decorated with smoked salmon and lemongrass; and no menu is complete without steak tartare, fish and chips, mushroom risotto, chicken curry, taco chips, stewed lamb shanks and sticky toffee pudding with double cream.

And now 'Modern Australian' has started to incorporate some of the most 'Ancient Australian' ingredients: kangaroo, emu, crocodile, lemon aspen, lillypillies, warrigal greens, wattleseeds and native peppers.

The classiest restaurants in Australia, which would have been French 20 years ago, now reflect this multicultural mix—Rockpool in Sydney has Thai and Middle Eastern inspirations, Tetsuya's in

Sydney blends Japanese and French styles, and Melbourne's Stephanie Alexander mingles Italian with Asian and Australian native touches.

So what might we consider to be Australia's National Dish in the 1990s, meaning the dish we most commonly cook at home and eat in non-trendy restaurants? The answer has to be Spaghetti Bolognese. And what is our national drink? Cappuccino. And what is the one word that best describes our lifestyle? 'Mediterranean', in the sense of warm, relaxed and hedonistic. Those are the three pillars of my contention that Australia is Italy's most successful colony. From the 1950s onwards it was the Italian invaders who did most to ensure that we became not only well-fed, but passionately interested in eating and drinking.

Now Australians have discovered that our range of soils and climates allows this country to grow anything that has ever existed elsewhere in the world, so that produce which has vanished from other countries because of pollution and overpopulation can be recreated here. And, finally, we have learned the cooking skills and the adventurous attitudes to give these ingredients the best treatment. The world is at the tip of our tongues.

74
tea

*t*he traditional Australian cure-all of 'a cup of tea and a good lie down' needs to be updated to 'a cup of coffee and good perk up'. The drink that had us addicted throughout the 19th century, consumed by genteel ladies from china cups and leathery swagmen from blackened tin mugs, has been losing its grip on us ever since World War Two. Blame it on the cultural imperialism of America, if you like, or possibly on the Italians—the first espresso machines were introduced in 1955 and we found out that coffee could actually taste good.

For the first 50 years of the Australian colony the standard weekly ration issued to itinerant farm labourers was called 'Ten, Ten, Two and a Quarter': ten pounds of flour, ten pounds of meat, two pounds of sugar and a quarter pound of tea. This suggests that throughout the 19th century every Australian was consuming 6 kilograms of tea a year. In 1903, a visiting British commentator, Percy Rowland, observed that 'a merciful Providence delayed the discovery of Australia until that of tea had rendered it inhabitable'.

The crucial year in our drinking history was 1979, when coffee on the way up passed tea on the way down. That year each Australian consumed 1.7 kilograms of tea and 1.7 kilograms of coffee. Nowadays we consume one kilo of tea per person per year, and 2.3 kilos of coffee. So every week, each adult Australian drinks six cups of coffee and two cups of tea.

Australians started growing their own teas in the 1970s. Of the 29 000 tonnes of tea we drink each year, 1000 tonnes is now locally grown—mostly in northern New South Wales and Queensland. Australian tea is said to be lower in caffeine and tannic acid than the imported stuff, which makes it healthier but less flavourful.

75
wine

*t*his nation has been making wine since 1816, and now the average Australian swallows 18.5 litres of it a year, which is a very moderate two and a half glasses a week for every man, woman and child. (By comparison, each Britisher drinks one and a half glasses a week and each French or Italian person nine glasses.) We export around 130 million litres a year to Britain, Sweden, New Zealand, North America and Japan. Surveys show most Australians drink wine at home, with a meal, on a Saturday.

The most familiar Australian white wine these days is chardonnay, usually aged in wooden barrels so it has an 'oaky' flavour. Our most familiar red style is cabernet sauvignon, so heavy and dark that at times it looks like purple syrup.

Our most fashionable wine-growing area is the Margaret River in Western Australia, with the Yarra Valley, near Melbourne, a close second. South Australian wines are seen as solid and reliable. Tasmanian wines are experimental. The least fashionable area is the Hunter Valley, north of Sydney.

The greatest Australian red is Penfold's Grange Hermitage, made in South Australia from shiraz and cabernet sauvignon grapes. But it's too expensive to appear on most restaurant wine lists. It raises the philosophical question of whether a wine can ever be worth $150 a bottle. The answer is: only if you don't drink it. For those with cellars, Grange is a wise investment. Best vintages are 1990, 1986, 1981, 1980, 1976 and 1971.

The title of greatest Australian white would be fought out among three oaky chardonnays: Petaluma (from the Adelaide Hills), Leeuwin Estate (Margaret River, WA) and Pierro (also Margaret River). Here are some more moderate suggestions . . .

☆ **WHITES** Coldstream Hills Reserve Chardonnay (Yarra Valley, Vic); Fermoy Semillon (Margaret River); Tyrell's Vat 1 Semillon (Hunter Valley, NSW); Leo Buring Leonay Riesling (Barossa Valley, SA); and Pipers Brook Riesling (Pipers River, Tasmania).

☆ **REDS** Henschke Hill of Grace (Eden Valley, SA); Penfolds Bin 707 Cabernet Sauvignon (Barossa); Rockford Basketpress Shiraz (Barossa); Leconfield Coonawarra Cabernet (Coonawarra, SA); Jasper Hill Shiraz (Heathcote, Vic); Mount Langi Ghiran Shiraz (Ararat, Vic); and Bannockburn Pinot Noir (Geelong, Vic).

76
bushfires and barbies

*a*ustralia has an almost mystical affinity with fire. Many native plants are dependent on regular bushfires to clear away undergrowth so the sun can reach them, or to help their pods burst and spread their seeds. So bushfires are a normal and necessary part of the Australian life cycle—which doesn't come as much comfort to those who lose their property or their families because they have built their homes in fire-prone areas.

The Australian bush is built to regenerate quickly—after the January 1994 fires which destroyed 90 per cent of the Royal National Park, south of Sydney, it took only two years for the park to look as dense and green as ever.

Before white settlement, the Aborigines used fire  for warfare, to landscape their territory and to promote the fruiting of certain edible plants. Modern Australians use it as part of a social and territorial ritual called The Barbecue. Before the year

1978, the Australian barbie was a clumsy brick and cement affair constructed by Dad in the backyard, with a slab of rusty metal stretched across as a hot-plate. Dad and his mates, wearing wittily decorated aprons, would throw slabs of red meat on the hot-plate, while Mum and the other wives brought salads and crisps from the kitchen.

But, in 1978, a pioneer named Ross McDonald brought from America a pod-shaped portable bar-becue called the Weber. He sold 500 000 of them over the next 15 years and revolutionised Australian barbecue behaviour. Suddenly even inner-city apart-ment dwellers could have a barbie on the balcony. And as our food consciousness grew, we started using the Webers for trendy ingredients such as marinated chicken on skewers. These days, some people even throw another prawn on the barbie.

77

our greatest disasters

☆ **ASH WEDNESDAY.** On 16 February 1983, bushfires broke out in the Adelaide Hills and in the Dandenong mountains near Melbourne. In four days, 1000 homes were destroyed and 72 people were killed.

☆ **THE THREDBO LANDSLIDE.** On 30 July, 1997, a landslide crushed two ski lodges at Thredbo, NSW, and killed 18 people.

☆ **THE DARWIN CYCLONE.** On 25 December, 1974, a cyclone called Tracy, with winds up to 250 kilometres an hour, struck Darwin and demolished most of its buildings. The damage led to $702 million in insurance bills, and 66 people were killed.

☆ **THE TASMAN BRIDGE COLLAPSE.** On 5 January, 1975, a bulk carrier rammed a pylon of the Tasman Bridge in Hobart, causing half of it to collapse. Five motorists and seven crew members were killed.

☆ **THE GRANVILLE TRAIN DISASTER.** On 18 January, 1977, a train left the rails near Sydney's Granville station, and rammed the supports of a bridge, which collapsed, crushing 83 people.

☆ **THE NEWCASTLE EARTHQUAKE.** On 28 December, 1989, the NSW coastal city of Newcastle was shaken by an earthquake which lasted 29 seconds, killed 13 people, and left 15 000 homeless.

☆ **THE PORT ARTHUR MASSACRE.** On 28 April, 1996, Martin Bryant, 29, shot dead 35 people in the tourist complex at the former convict settlement of Port Arthur, Tasmania. He was sentenced to life imprisonment.

☆ **THE MILPERRA MASSACRE.** On 2 September 1984, seven people were killed and 21 wounded in a shootout between rival motorbike gangs in the carpark of the Viking Hotel, Milperra, a suburb of Sydney.

☆ **THE HODDLE STREET MASSACRE.** On 9 August 1987, Julian Knight, who was 19 and unemployed, killed seven people and wounded 19 by firing off various automatic weapons in Hoddle Street, Melbourne.

☆ **THE BACKPACKER MURDERS.** During 1992 and 1993, seven bodies, either stabbed or shot to death, were found buried in Belanglo State Forest, near Berrima, NSW. They were mainly European tourists who had disappeared between 1989 and 1992. A local man named Ivan Milat was sentenced to life imprisonment for the murders.

78
big business

*a*ny shortlist of Australia's major moneymakers
would have to include:

☆ **AMP** (the Australian Mutual Provident Society),
founded in 1849 and now Australia's biggest
insurance company and most influential investor.
It manages assets of $80 billion and has $178
billion insured, earning $6.7 billion a year from
premiums and $4.3 billion from investments.

☆ **BHP** (The Broken Hill Proprietary Co),
Australia's biggest company, founded to mine
silver and lead in 1885, with annual revenues
around $20 billion from the sale of minerals,
steel and oil. It employs 60 000 people and
made a profit of $1.04 billion in 1996, but
angered many Australians by announcing in
1997 that it would close its operations in
Newcastle and put thousands out of work.

☆ **COLES MYER**, our biggest retailer, founded in
1914 and now running a national chain of
department stores and supermarkets with
annual sales of $19 billion and a profit in 1996
of $280 million. It is also Australia's biggest
private employer, with 135 000 staff.

☆ **THE NATIONAL AUSTRALIA BANK (NAB)**, Australia's biggest bank, formed in 1981 from the merger of two banks that started in Sydney in 1834 and 1858. It has the highest assets of any Australian company—$147 billion—and made a profit in 1996 of $1.96 billion (15 per cent more than the previous year).

☆ **NEWS CORP**, Rupert Murdoch's international media organisation based in Australia, which earned $14 billion in 1996 and made a profit of $1.02 billion.

☆ **RTZ-CRA**, a mining conglomerate, has annual revenue of $11 billion and profit of $1.3 billion, employing 53 000 people.

Australia's richest individuals, according to *Business Review Weekly* magazine, are: 1. Kerry Packer (see chapter 80); 2. Frank Lowy, whose company, Westfield Holdings, creates shopping centres, and whose personal fortune is $1.4 billion; 3. Richard Pratt, whose Visy Industries makes paper packaging ($1.3 billion); 4. Harry Triguboff, whose Meriton Group builds cheap houses ($1.2 billion); 5. David Hains, whose diverse investments give him assets worth $950 million. Australia's richest woman is Janet Holmes a Court, whose vast cattle properties in Western Australia and theatres in London make her worth $200 million.

79
Rupert Murdoch

*a*ustralia's most influential export has been Rupert Murdoch, boss of the media company News Corporation. Australians note that he is a US citizen when he embarrasses us and Australian-born when he achieves a financial coup.

In Britain he is nicknamed 'The Dirty Digger' for allegedly encouraging inaccuracy, sensationalism and invasion of privacy in his newspapers (notably the *Sun* and the *News of the World*). In America he has been accused (by *GQ* magazine) of introducing 'a medieval emphasis on boobs, bottoms and bodily humours' via his tabloid newspapers and the programs on his Fox television network. (The *GQ* article said Murdoch has exploited 'the most significant trait shared by Australia and America', which is 'anti-elitism—the passing off of remunerative junk culture as the people's will, and the dismissal of intellectualism as uppityness'.) In Asia, where he owns the major satellite television suppliers, he is accused of destroying local cultures and imposing American standardisation.

Murdoch, who was born in 1931, owns 75 per cent of Australia's newspapers, including the biggest-selling paper in the country, the *Sunday*

Telegraph (720 000 copies), the national daily the *Australian*, Melbourne's *Herald Sun*, the *Northern Territory News*, and Brisbane's *Courier Mail*. He owns half of Ansett Airlines.

Murdoch's News Corp has signed up most of Australia's top rugby league players to play in a competition called Super League, which is promoted enthusiastically by his newspapers. He is a key investor in new forms of television, telephone and computer communications, which will ensure his son Lachlan and daughter Elisabeth continue the Murdoch dominance of world media into the 21st century.

80
Kerry Packer

*t*he richest individual in Australia is Kerry Packer—worth $3.9 billion at last estimate. He owns Australia's top rating TV network Channel Nine and a magazine empire that includes Australia's two top selling publications *Women's Weekly* (805 000 copies a month) and *Woman's Day* (661 000 copies a week). He has interests in professional cricket, football and polo, chemical and mining companies, cattle properties, ski resorts and the Melbourne casino.

In 1983 he was investigated as part of a Royal Commission into tax avoidance and drug trafficking, because of his habit of carrying large quantities of cash with him. It appeared that the money was to fund his hobby of gambling (he's been reported to win and lose millions of dollars

in a weekend at the racetrack and at the blackjack tables of international casinos). The Royal Commission found no evidence of wrongdoing but, in the course of it, Packer received the nickname 'The

Goanna' and developed a hatred of investigative journalists.

During the mid 1990s Australians were diverted by vigorous competition between Packer and Rupert Murdoch for control of professional rugby league, and by an apparent feud between Packer and the Labor leader Paul Keating, who accused Packer of using his media influence to support the Liberal leader, John Howard. After Howard was elected Prime Minister, he tried to change the media ownership laws in a way which could have resulted in Packer being able to retain the Nine Network while taking over the Fairfax newspaper company, publisher of Australia's main quality dailies *The Age* and *The Sydney Morning Herald*.

The dynasty, begun by Frank Packer in the 1930s, and expanded by Kerry from the 1960s, will continue with Kerry's son James.

81
dangers

*t*he most alarming creatures you're likely to encounter if you try to be too adventurous in Australia are . . .

☆ **SEA WASPS**. Over the past 100 years, this box jellyfish has stung to death about 60 people swimming in Australia's northern tropical waters between October and May. They are almost transparent, with sticky stinging tentacles three metres long. Experienced surfers wear pantyhose if they have to enter stinger-infested waters.

☆ **SHARKS**. The species most likely to attack humans in Australian waters are the whaler (or bull) shark, the white pointer (or great white) shark and the tiger shark. There have been about 400 deaths from shark attacks in Australian waters this century, but a swimmer in Australia is 50 times more likely to die from drowning than from a shark bite.

Exotic Fashion Items ☆ 46
The Saltwater Crocodile
Bodysuit

☆ **SNAKES.** Australia has more deadly species than any other country, with the worst three being the taipan, the tiger snake and the death adder. Since the 1970s around 300 Australian snake-bite victims a year have been injected with antivenom and two or three people die every year because they don't get the antivenom in time.

☆ **SALTWATER CROCODILES.** The largest saltwater crocodile caught in Australia was 8.6 metres long, but mostly they don't exceed five metres. Either way you're unlikely to survive an encounter with one, so it's not advisable to swim in unpopulated rivers or swamps along the northern Australian coastline between King Sound, Western Australia, and Hervey Bay, Queensland. Since 1970 there has been an average of one crocodile attack on a human each year.

☆ **SPIDERS.** Of Australia's 1400 identified species, the most venomous are the funnel-web (found mainly around Sydney) and the redback (found everywhere). Each was recorded as killing 13 people between the time white settlers started noting such things and the development of antivenin in the 1970s. In the 1990s, funnel-web bites have been rare, and there are about 100 redback bites a year, none fatal.

✫ **THE PARASITIC BUSH TICK.** The world's most infectious tick, it feeds on human blood and has killed about 20 people this century.

✫ **THE BLUE-RINGED OCTOPUS.** Found all round the coastline, they are only a couple of centimetres across, but their beaks are full of venom which can paralyse and kill within 12 hours if the victim is not given artificial respiration. There have been only two confirmed killings this century by blue-ringed octopus (which are actually brown until they get angry).

✫ **BULLDOG ANTS.** The most dangerous ants in the world, they are big (up to 4 centimetres long) with long mandibles with which they grip their victim while injecting their sting. They are found all over Australia and are held responsible for three deaths, the latest a Victorian farmer in 1988.

✫ **THE STINGING TREE.** In rainforests along Australia's eastern coastline grow three species of stinging tree, which have large leaves covered with sticky hairs. Brushing against them causes agonising pain and swelling in the groin and armpits. The pain can last for weeks, but the sting is not usually fatal.

✫ **STONEFISH.** If you're walking in the water at a beach in the northern half of Australia, hope you don't tread on a stonefish, which sits on the bottom and will inject you with one of the 13 poisonous spines along its back.

☆ **BLUEBOTTLES**. Not fatal, but a serious summer nuisance, these jellyfish inflict painful stings from their long tentacles. They are sometimes blown onto beaches in clusters by strong winds.

☆ **CROWN OF THORNS STARFISH.** Not dangerous to humans, but a voracious consumer of coral polyps, devastating the Great Barrier Reef and endangering one of Australia's top tourist attractions.

82
stirrers

a ustralians affectionately use the terms 'ratbag' or 'stirrer' for idealists who raise provocative ideas or campaign for social change. Some of our favourite troublesome thinkers are . . .

☆ **BOB BROWN**. Trained as a doctor, he has devoted his life to political agitation for environmental causes, particularly saving the wilderness areas of Tasmania. He was elected as a Green senator for Tasmania in 1996.

☆ **HELEN CALDICOTT**. A Melbourne doctor who decided to save lives by going to America and forming Physicians for Social Responsibility to attack nuclear weapons and nuclear energy, and who became a successful nuisance to the US government. She has now broadened her campaigning to include environmental and population causes.

☆ **GERMAINE GREER**. A Melbourne-born writer now living in England, she stunned the world in 1970 with *The Female Eunuch*, an analysis of the historical oppression of women. Since then she has regularly surprised her fans by, at different times, condemning immorality, welcoming menopause and attacking boring women poets.

☆ **DONALD HORNE**. Author, in 1964, of the ironically titled *The Lucky Country*, which attacked Australian materialism and complacency, he now organises Ideas conferences and campaigns to make Australia a republic.

☆ **BARRY JONES**. Best known in the 1960s as an argumentative quiz champion on the TV show 'Pick a Box', he became the Labor Government's Minister for Science during the 1980s, set up the Commission for the Future, and ended up National President of the Labor Party.

☆ **JACK MUNDEY**. As head of the Sydney branch of the Builders Labourers' Federation in the 1970s, he urged unionists to follow their conscience in refusing to work on projects that might damage historic buildings or fragile environments. He was removed from power, but his term 'green ban' has stayed in our language.

☆ **RICHARD NEVILLE**. A 1960s proponent of experimentation with sex, drugs and rock and roll, he founded the satire magazine *Oz* in Australia and then in Britain, was sentenced to jail in 1971 for publishing material likely 'to corrupt morals', but freed on appeal, and is now settled in domestic bliss just outside Sydney.

☆ **PHILIP NITSCHKE**. A campaigner for the right of terminally ill people to seek euthanasia, he helped four cancer sufferers to give themselves fatal doses of drugs after the Northern Territory legalised euthanasia in 1996. When federal parliament overruled the Northern Territory law, Nitschke began work on a machine which would allow terminal patients to place themselves in a coma until their deaths.

☆ **CHARLES PERKINS.** In the early 1960s he led the first 'freedom rides' to protest about discrimination against Aborigines in NSW country towns, and went on to head the federal government's Aboriginal Affairs Department.

☆ **PETER SINGER.** His 1975 book *Animal Liberation* argued that animals have the same rights as humans, and should not be eaten or used as slaves or pets (though they can be 'companions'). It started a worldwide movement. He now runs the Centre for Human Bioethics at Monash University, Melbourne.

☆ **BARBARA THIERING.** A lecturer in Divinity at Sydney University, she published a book in 1993 called *Jesus the Man*, which argued that Jesus was naturally conceived and did not die on the cross. Hardly had the traditional Christian outrage died down when she published *Jesus of the Apocalypse*, which portrays Jesus and his followers as political activists who made Judaism the most influential force of the first century.

83
transformations

*t*he two biggest changes in the everyday lives of Australians this century were the move to decimal currency in 1966, and the move to the metric system in 1975. Australians still need some idea of the bizarre earlier systems to understand literary references and the language of people over 40. Before 1966, Australia's money consisted of pounds, shillings and pence. There were two halfpennies (pronounced haypenny) in a penny, 12 pennies in a shilling (also known as a bob), 20 shillings in a pound (also known as a quid) and 21 shillings in a guinea. At the changeover, ten shillings became a dollar.

The imperial system of weights and measures that operated before 1975 was even weirder than the money. There were 12 inches in a foot, 3 feet in a yard and 1760 yards in a mile. (A yard was roughly a metre.) All schoolkids learned that a length of five and a half yards was called a rod, pole or perch, but nobody ever knew what to measure with it. Horse races

(Imperial Cartoon)
3 feet in a yard

183

were run in furlongs (220 yards). An acre was an area of 4840 square yards. In weights, there were 16 ounces in a pound (which was roughly half a kilogram). Temperatures were measured in a scale called fahrenheit, which ran from a freezing point of 32 to a boiling point of 212. So instead of having temperatures in the 30s, a typical Australian summer in the 1960s had temperatures in the 90s.

Liquids were measured in pints (about half a litre), with eight pints to the gallon. So your Holden was doing well if it did 40 miles to the gallon of petrol. These days it would do 15 kilometres to the litre, but at least we haven't started referring to petrol as gas.

84
investments

*a*ccording to the research organisation Access
Economics, the assets most likely to grow
in value between now and the year 2001 are
bottles of Australian red wine (Penfold's 1971
Grange, for example, tripled its value in 25 years),
international and Australian bonds, rare coins,
rare stamps, Australian paintings, houses in Brisbane, and a plate entitling you to own a taxi in
Sydney or Melbourne. Access based this on the
performance of these items over the early 1990s.
They listed as investments which are performing
at below the inflation rate, or actually declining
in value: thoroughbred horses, gold, diamonds,
Melbourne houses, rural land.

Now, when we talk about rare coins, the one
Australians most often fantasise about finding in a
jar in their grandmother's house is a 1930 penny.
Only about 3000 of these were made by the Melbourne Mint because nobody was spending money
in the Depression. Nowadays a 1930 penny in good
condition could fetch $50 000. Its equivalent for
philatelists is the 1854 fourpenny stamp from
Western Australia, on which the black swan was
printed upside down by mistake. Several hundred of

these were produced at the time, but only 15 have turned up in the modern world so far and, in 1989, one of them sold for $114 000.

Of course, there's always business investment, but here's a lesson . . . *The Guinness Book of Records* says Australia's biggest corporate loss was $2.25 billion announced by Bond Corporation for the year to 30 June 1990. The company's founder, Alan Bond, resigned from the board two days before this figure was announced. A major part of the corporation's earnings came from beer-making. So if you can't make money selling beer in Australia, there's no security in anything.

85
our artists

*i*f you're wandering through a junk shop and you happen upon a painting by Rupert Bunny or Sidney Nolan, pick it up instantly, because they are among the hottest names in Australian painting at the moment, as judged by the prices they fetch at auction. Bunny did most of his landscape work in Melbourne in the 1920s and died in 1947. His *Une Nuit de Canicule* sold for $1.25 million in 1988, but was destroyed in a fire soon afterwards. Nolan, best known for his Ned Kelly series in the 1940s, died in 1991, and his set of nine small paintings called *Riverbend II* fetched $1 022 181 in 1993. The highest price ever obtained for an Australian painting was $1 982 500 in 1996 for Eugene von Guerard's *View of Geelong*. Von Guerard, an immigrant from Austria, painted it in 1856. The buyer's name was kept secret by the auctioneers, but it was thought to be either Kerry Packer or Rupert Murdoch.

The other most profitably auctioned names of the 1990s are Arthur Streeton, Russell Drysdale, Fred McCubbin and Arthur Boyd. Boyd was named Australian of the Year in 1995, partly for his body of work—of which a desert series called *The Half*

Caste Bride is best known—and partly because he donated to the nation his property called Bundanon, on the Shoalhaven River south of Sydney. Some more names to know in Australian art are:

☆ **KOONALDA CAVE.** The painters' names are unknown, but 20 000 years ago they scratched designs on the wall of a cave that is now beneath the Nullarbor Plain in South Australia. It's the oldest art in Australia and probably the world. A little later—some 12 000 years ago—another group of unknown painters stencilled the shapes of their hands on the walls of Ballawine Cave, on the banks of the Maxwell River in south-west Tasmania.

☆ **COLIN LANCELEY,** a pioneer of 1960s pop art, still producing lavish surprises.

☆ **NORMAN LINDSAY,** an illustrator for books and magazines who shocked the Sydney puritans from the early 1900s with his drawings and paintings of satyrs and voluptuous women.

☆ **ALBERT NAMATJIRA,** a watercolourist of Central Australian landscapes, who died in 1959.

☆ **MARGARET PRESTON,** a 1920s modernist specialising in still lifes of Australian wildflowers.

☆ **TOM ROBERTS,** who founded the first Australian school of painting at Heidelberg near Melbourne in the 1880s, and specialised in bush imagery. He inspired Hans Heysen, Fred McCubbin and Arthur Streeton.

☆ **BRETT WHITELEY**, as famous for his drug addiction and romantic adventures as for his vast ocean images, who died in 1992.

☆ **YIRAWALA**, a traditional bark painter from Arnhem Land in the Northern Territory, who died in 1976.

The most important art prize in Australia is the Archibald, announced at the Art Gallery of NSW each January. Since it requires a portrait of a person distinguished in arts or letters, it regularly provokes controversy, particularly about what constitutes a portrait.

And the most financially successful Australian artist of all time is Ken Done, whose sunny designs cover clothing, teatowels, handbags, cushions and umbrellas, and who sells particularly well to Japanese visitors.

Ken Done represents popular taste. A further insight is offered by a list of the most successful shows toured by Art Exhibitions Australia, which packages most of the visiting blockbusters: 1. Gold of the Pharoahs (1988), seen by more than 900 000 people; 2. China's Entombed Warriors (1983), seen by 800 000; 3. Golden Summers (1986), a collection of 19th century Australian paintings, seen by 550 000; 4. Rubens and the Italian Renaissance (1992), seen by 450 000; 5. Renoir (1995), seen by 400 000.

86
the flag

*e*very couple of years there's a burst of enthusiasm for changing the Australian flag. Unofficial polls are run; new designs are shown (usually without the Union Jack, and often with a red semi-circle to represent Ayers Rock); the monarchists get outraged; and nothing happens. It's all too difficult, the governments say, apparently forgetting that in 1901 the newly formed Australian government was able to run a flag competition which attracted 32 823 entries. The judges chose a design showing a five-star constellation called the Southern Cross on a dark blue background, with a Union Jack in the top left corner to symbolise our historic ties with Britain.

Whatever happens to Australia's flag, it is unlikely to lose the Southern Cross because, after

the moon, it's the most easily recognisable image in our night sky and a frequent reference point in patriotic poetry. It was the motif on the flag that flew over the Eureka Stockade where, in 1854, a group of gold miners staged a protest strike against excessive licence fees being charged by the government of Victoria. Eureka was the nearest Australia has come to a revolution against authority, so its symbol—the Southern Cross—appeals to Australians of progressive inclination.

But what is the Southern Cross? A bunch of stars which were over the northern hemisphere three thousand years ago, and were visible on the horizon on the day of Christ's crucifixion (which some may have found pretty spooky). As the earth has changed its tilt over time, the constellation called Crux Australis has become the monopoly of southerners.

It may look like a pattern to us but, out in space, the five stars are nowhere near each other. The nearest is 59 light years from earth and the furthest is 425 light years off. So there's no way to tell if they have planets, let alone whether there's life on the Southern Cross. But the good news is that one of the two 'pointer' stars just above the cross, Alpha Centauri, is the closest star to the earth—a mere 4.3 light years away.

87
the anthem

*M*ost adult Australians were brought up to sing a song called 'God Save the Queen' at school every day and to stand up for it before the curtains opened at the movies or the theatre. It was the national anthem of both Britain and Australia.

In 1973, the Labor Government of Gough Whitlam held a contest to create a distinctly Australian anthem, but the judges concluded that none of the 1400 entries was good enough, and that we'd be better off reworking a traditional tune. An opinion poll in 1974, and a referendum in 1977, showed that most Australians had strong affection for two songs—'Waltzing Matilda', written by Banjo Paterson in 1895, and 'Advance Australia Fair', written by Peter Dodds McCormick in 1878. In the referendum, 'Advance Australia Fair' got 2.9 million votes, 'Waltzing Matilda' got 1.9 million and 'God Save the Queen' got 1.3 million.

But there were problems with the words of 'Advance Australia', which began 'Australia's sons let us

192

rejoice' and turned decidedly militaristic in the second verse. It was not until 1984 that a rewritten version (with the second verse dropped) was declared to be the national anthem. This is it:

Australians all let us rejoice,
For we are young and free;
We've golden soil and wealth for toil;
Our home is girt by sea;
Our land abounds in nature's gifts
Of beauty rich and rare;
In history's page, let every stage Advance
Australia Fair.
In joyful strains then let us sing, Advance
Australia Fair.

Beneath our radiant Southern Cross
We'll toil with hearts and hands;
To make this Commonwealth of ours
Renowned of all the lands;
For those who've come across the seas
We've boundless plains to share;
With courage let us all combine To Advance
Australia Fair.
In joyful strains then let us sing, Advance
Australia Fair.

It's probably no more embarrassing than most national anthems, and when you consider the alternative—a song about a suicidal sheep stealer in largely incomprehensible dialect—we have reason to rejoice.

88
honours

*t*he monarch of England, on the recommendation of the federal or a state government, used
to confer knighthoods and other honours such as
the CBE, OBE and MBE (Commander, Officer and
Member of the British Empire) on Australians
thought to have done community service. Many
people suspected that you could buy a knighthood
by contributing a suitable sum to the political party
in power, and one rumour told of the businessman
who won his knighthood in a poker game with a
state premier.

In 1975, the Whitlam Labor Government introduced a separate Australian system of honours,
asserting our independence from the British Empire.
From then on, whenever Liberal governments were
in power, they recommended the Imperial honours,
while Labor governments awarded the local
honours. Finally, in 1989, Queen Elizabeth got sick
of this erratic behaviour and told Australian governments to stop asking her for honours. The last
royal knighthood conferred in Australia was recommended by the Queensland Government in
1988, and went to the Commissioner of Police,
Terence Lewis. In 1991 Sir Terence was stripped of

his knighthood after being convicted of corruption.

Now Australia has one system of honours which, according to a survey in 1995, is understood by only 44 per cent of Australians. The top honour is called Companion of the Order of Australia (AC) 'for eminent achievement or merit of the highest degree in service to Australia or to humanity at large'. A maximum of 25 of these are handed out each year, either on Australia Day (January 26) or on the Queen's Birthday holiday (June 14). Recent recipients have included Elizabeth Evatt, the first judge of the Australian Family Court; Neal Blewett, a former federal Health Minister and Australian High Commissioner to London; Nick Greiner, a former NSW Premier; and Tony Fitzgerald, who ran the investigation into corruption in Queensland which lost Terence Lewis his knighthood. Brian Burke, a former Premier of Western Australia, got an AC but was stripped of it in 1993 after being convicted of defrauding the state. The President of Turkey and the Prime Minister of Greece each received an honorary AC in the 1990s.

Next down the ladder is Officer of the Order of Australia (AO), then Member of the Order of Australia (AM), and Medal of the Order of Australia (OAM). Each year the federal government also announces an Australian of the Year. These have included Fred Hollows, an eye surgeon who halved the rate of blindness among Australia's outback Aborigines; Mandawuy Yunupingu, a teacher and leader of the Aboriginal rock group Yothu Yindi; and Kay Cottee, the first woman to sail a yacht solo around the world.

Anyone can nominate anyone for one of these awards, on a form which will be sent to you if you phone Government House in Canberra. Your nomination will be checked out by a committee of public servants.

89
our music

a ustralians were outraged in 1995 when the Rock and Roll Hall of Fame in Cleveland, Ohio, announced its 'definitive' list of 'The 500 Most Influential Rock Songs of All Time'. Only three Australian songs were included (or four, if you stretch a point and include 'Stayin Alive' by the Bee Gees, who began their singing career here). They were 'Highway to Hell' and 'Back in Black' by AC/DC, and 'Beds Are Burning' by Midnight Oil.

Certainly AC/DC has been our most internationally successful heavy-metal band (selling 60 million albums worldwide) and Midnight Oil offer a worthy mixture of rock and environmental activism. But Australians wanted to know what happened to 'You're the Voice' by John Farnham, 'Working Class Man' by Jimmy Barnes, 'Electric Blue' by Icehouse, 'Eagle Rock' by Daddy Cool, 'Pub with No Beer' by Slim Dusty, 'The Real Thing' by Russell Morris, 'Evie' by Stevie Wright, 'Love Is In The Air' by John Paul Young, 'Land Down Under' by Men At Work, and 'Tie Me Kangaroo Down, Sport' by Rolf Harris. That's not to mention international bestsellers such as 'I Should Be So Lucky' by Kylie Minogue, and 'Shaddap You Face' by Joe Dolce (four million copies).

They were also distressed at the absence of such 1950s icons as Johnny O'Keefe and Col Joye, 1960s icons Billy Thorpe, the Seekers and the Easybeats, 1970s icons Little River Band and Skyhooks, 1980s icons INXS, Nick Cave, Crowded House, Australian Crawl, Mental As Anything and Split Enz, and 1990s icons such as silverchair and Yothu Yindi.

That's just the beginning of a shortlist of songs and performers that live in the memory of pop-oriented Australians. Australian jazz buffs point proudly at the work of trumpeters Bob Barnard and James Morrison, pianist Graeme Bell, vibist John Sangster, and multi-instrumentalist Don Burrows.

Classically minded Australians have fewer international successes to reflect upon. Percy Grainger is our most familiar composer, as much for his eccentric lifestyle (a piano prodigy obsessed with bondage and his mother) as for his compositions ('In An English Country Garden', which he called a 'frippery', made him a fortune). Grainger became a US citizen in 1914 and died in New York in 1961. In modern times, our key composers are Peter Sculthorpe and Nigel Butterly, and our world-class classical musicians include the pianist Roger Woodward, the guitarist John Williams and the French horn virtuoso Barry Tuckwell, described by the *Grove Dictionary of Music* as 'the leading horn player of his generation'.

Nellie Melba was the first of our classical singers to make international waves, dominating the opera houses of Europe and America in the 1890s and then doing a legendary series of farewell concerts in Australia during the 1920s. Peach Melba and Melba toast are named after her, but she was not a sweet dish—the author Max Harris described her as 'the all time champion Australian bitch ... demanding, dictatorial, ruthless, capricious, inconsiderate, tight-fisted, stingy, mean, ungrateful, pathologically jealous, publicity hungry and supremely egotistical'.

Australians were rather more fond of Gladys Moncrieff, who toured the world in operettas during the 1930s and outdid Melba with a series of farewells that lasted from 1952 to 1961. At the height of her career, it was said that Sydney had three assets: 'Our harbour, our bridge and our Glad'.

More recently Joan Sutherland has inherited the Melba musical mantle (and had a chocolate pudding named after her at Sydney's Regent Hotel). And the eccentric pianist David Helfgott, hero of the movie *Shine*, has been hugely successful with concerts and albums in America and Britain, despite critical panning.

In popular music at the moment, Australian tastes run mostly to whining American women. The top ten best selling albums of 1996 included work by Alanis Morissette, Celine Dion, Toni Childs and Mariah Carey. The only Australian in the top ten was John Farnham, unless you count Crowded House (really New Zealanders).

90
what we buy

O n the principle that you are what you buy, we can gain considerable insight into the Australian identity by looking at the nation's favourite products. In 1996, the Nielsen organisation reported that Australians spent more than $100 million on each of the following brands in supermarkets: 1. Coca Cola. 2. Nescafe. 3. Longbeach cigarettes. 4. Winfield cigarettes. 5. Peter Jackson cigarettes. 6. Pedigree Pal dog food. 7. Kraft cheese. 8. Tip Top bread. 9. Sorbent toilet paper. 10. Buttercup bread. 11. Huggies nappies. 12. Whiskas cat food. 13. Cadbury block chocolate. 14. Arnott's biscuits. (You might assume from this that Australians are big time smokers, and indeed we do consume 35 billion cigarettes a year—the equivalent of six a day for every man, woman and child. In fact, 3.1 million adult Australians—23 per cent of women and 27 per cent of men—are smokers).

Based on Nielsen's top 100 best selling products, here's what the typical Australian family (two parents, two teenage kids) did yesterday ... They woke up and headed for the bathroom, where they wiped with Sorbent toilet tissue, showered with

Palmolive soap, shampooed with Pantene and deodorised with Rexona. Dad shaved with a Gillette razor, Mum put on her Razzamatazz pantihose, daughter put in a Libra tampon and son lit up his first Winfield of the day.

For breakfast, Mum and Dad had Weet-Bix and the kids had Kelloggs cornflakes, followed by toasted Tip Top sliced white bread, spread with Meadow Lea margarine and Vegemite. They drank Berri orange juice and Nescafe with CSR white sugar. They fed the dog Pal and the cat Whiskas. Before leaving for work, Mum popped a Panadol in case she might get a headache, and did a wash with Omo. Dad popped an amoxycillin for his throat infection.

For morning tea, the parents had Bega cheddar on Arnott's Saos. The kids had Yoplait yoghurt. For lunch they all ate San Remo pasta sprinkled with Kraft cheese, and drank Coca Cola, though Mum had Diet Coke, which allowed her to eat two pieces of Cadbury's chocolate. For afternoon tea, Mum and Dad had Arnott's Tim Tams, the son had Smith's potato chips, and the daughter had Thins. With dinner they ate Edgell canned vegetables, Birds Eye frozen peas, Rosella tomato sauce, Golden Circle canned pineapple and Street's ice cream. They brushed with Colgate Fluorogard and went to bed. At his girlfriend's house, the son used an Ansell Affinity condom (regular).

There is, however, one big mystery in our purchasing patterns during the 1990s. The Nielsen survey showed that every year Australians are buying more and more rubber gloves (mostly made by the Ansell rubber company). We bought 35 million pairs in 1995, which means that every man, woman and child in Australia is getting at least two pairs of rubber gloves every year. Don't ask me what they're doing with them.

91
our scientists

*i*n the early 1990s, the Federal Government declared its desire to make Australia 'the clever country' by encouraging people to stay at school and university longer, though this was later under-cut by the introduction of higher university fees. We hadn't been doing too badly this century before we started calling ourselves clever, having won ten Nobel prizes for scientific and medical research. Our most significant scientists have been . . .

☆ **MACFARLANE BURNET,** a Melbourne boy whose work on bacterial viruses pioneered biotechnology and genetic engineering. He was the first to suggest (in 1949) how tissues and organs could be transplanted from one creature to another, and shared the Nobel Prize for Medicine in 1960 for 'the discovery of acquired immunological tolerance'.

☆ **JOHN CORNFORTH,** who has been deaf since his birth in Sydney in 1917. His work in Britain on molecular organic chemistry led him to sharing the Nobel Prize for Chemistry in 1975 for 'researches on the stereochemistry of enzyme-catalysed reactions'.

✩ **PETER DOHERTY**, a Brisbane doctor (working in America) who won the Nobel Prize for Medicine in 1996 for research he did in the 1970s on the body's immune response, which helped with organ transplants. He was named Australian of the Year in 1997.

✩ **JOHN ECCLES**, a Melbourne boy who specialised in the study of the spine and brain, shared the Nobel Prize for Medicine in 1963 for 'establishing the relationship of nerve cells and repolarisation of a cell's membrane'.

✩ **HOWARD FLOREY**, an Adelaide boy who became Professor of Pathology at Oxford University and developed the world's first antibiotic. He shared the Nobel Prize for medicine in 1945 for 'the discovery of penicillin and its curative effects in various infectious diseases'.

✩ **MARK OLIPHANT**, an Adelaide physicist whose work in Britain during World War Two led to advances in radar and to the development of the hydrogen bomb, although he condemned this use of nuclear energy and later campaigned for disarmament.

92
cuddly rats

*t*here once was an Australian animal known as the rabbit-eared bandicoot. It was cute and furry but, because people had chopped down much of its habitat and rabbits kept eating its food, it was an endangered species. Nobody seemed to care.

Then some clever zoologists gave it a change of name, drawing on an Aboriginal word, and the rabbit-eared bandicoot became the bilby. Its plight got media attention, the confectionery industry started making chocolate replicas of it, and a movement started to replace the Easter Bunny with the Easter Bilby as part of children's festivities during March.

But what about all the other native creatures which have been disappearing since European settlement in Australia? An estimated 17 types of land mammal which flourished in 1788 are now extinct, 22 are in danger of extinction, and another 80 are vulnerable.

Endangered Species #57: Scientists who study echidnas

A group of CSIRO scientists think a bit of repackaging might help. They have started a campaign to substitute Aboriginal words for the 'uninspiring, unwieldy and downright ugly' names assigned to Australian animals in the 19th century. They argue that it's impossible to inspire public sympathy for animals with names like the black-footed tree rat, the large rock rat, and the dusky hopping mouse. 'These animals are unique but the public associate the words rat and mouse with vermin and disease,' says Steve Morton from the CSIRO's division of Wildlife and Ecology in Canberra. So please memorise the following replacements . . .

☆ Water rat: **rakali.**
☆ Plains rat: **palyoora.**
☆ Greater stick-nest rat: **wopilkara.**
☆ Dusky hopping mouse: **wilkinti.**
☆ Brush-tailed rabbit rat: **pakooma.**
☆ Black-footed tree rat: **djintamoonga.**
☆ Large rock rat: **djookooropa.**
☆ Western chestnut mouse: **moolpoo.**
☆ Bush rat: **mootit.**
☆ Long-haired rat: **mayaroo.**

93
our architects

*t*he Aborigines were not inclined to build for posterity, so the earliest human structures still visible in Australia date from after the British arrival. Our oldest house is Elizabeth Farm at Parramatta, near Sydney—a brick cottage built by convicts in 1793 for John and Elizabeth Macarthur.

The first fashionable builder was Francis Greenway, a convicted forger who arrived in 1814 and was appointed Civil Architect by Governor Macquarie. He designed 40 public structures of which the Hyde Park Barracks in Macquarie Street, Sydney, and St Matthew's Church, Windsor, are the best surviving examples. Greenway was arrogant and argumentative, which got him dismissed in 1822 by Governor Brisbane, but which started a continuing tradition among Australian architects. Other names to know . . .

☆ **WALTER BURLEY GRIFFIN**, an American who trained in Chicago under Frank Lloyd Wright and won the design competition for the national capital, Canberra, in 1912, but resigned from the project in 1920 after a fight with the bureaucrats. He went on to design the

NSW towns of Leeton and Griffith, the
Melbourne suburbs of Heidelberg and
Eaglemont, and the Sydney suburb of
Castlecrag.

☆ **ROBIN BOYD**, a Melbourne architect who
was better known for his book, *The Australian
Ugliness*, published in 1960, than for any
particular building. He was an influential critic
of the suburban sprawl and of the
derivativeness of our streetscapes. But he
couldn't stop Australians building a million
red-brick bungalows.

☆ **GLEN MURCUTT**, who turned the tin shed
into an art form. He took up Boyd's challenge
and designed houses, farms and restaurants to
suit the Australian climate and landscape, often
with corrugated steel roofs and glass louvre
windows.

☆ **HARRY SEIDLER**, a Vienna-born, Sydney-
based architect who specialises in austere
skyscrapers in the Modern (ie 1950s) style.
Sydney's Australia Square Tower, Blues Point
Tower and MLC Centre are his work.

☆ **PHILIP COX**, a specialist in big public
structures, often using steel cables, such as the
Sydney Football Stadium, the Darling Harbour
Exhibition Centre and Yulara Tourist Resort
near Ayers Rock. He is the key figure in
designing for the Olympics in 2000.

94

our mags

a ustralians read—or at any rate, skim—more magazines per head than any other nation. We spend $765 million a year on them, which means that every man, woman, and child buys 15 magazines a year. *Women's Weekly* (which is actually a monthly) sells 805 000 a month. Then the list goes like this: *Woman's Day* (661 000 a week), *Reader's Digest* (500 000 a month), *New Idea* (484 000 a week), *That's Life* (469 000 a week), *Better Homes and Gardens* (340 000 a month) and *TV Week* (316 000 a week).

In recent years, the mass magazine market has been slowly declining, as the audience has grown tired of sensationalised gossip and has fragmented to 'niche' magazines. The fastest growing glossies in the late 1990s are personal computer mags, *Girlfriend* and *TV Hits* (for teenyboppers), *Marie Claire* (for fashionable women), *Good Taste* (for people who still cook at home) and *Gourmet Traveller* (for rich hedonists).

95
nearest neighbours

*n*ew Zealand occupies for Australia the same role that Ireland occupies for Britain, or Belgium for France, or Canada for the USA. We make jokes about New Zealanders, we patronise them, we take holidays there—and we let 500 000 of them come here each year to spend money and work as waiters, ABC news reporters and transvestite prostitutes in Sydney's Kings Cross. And we happily claim their most successful exports as honorary Australians: such as Jane Campion, writer-director of *The Piano*, and Sam Neill, star of *Jurassic Park*.

There is every good reason for New Zealand's two islands to become the seventh and eighth states of Australia since our countries are virtually amalgamated anyway, but the Kiwis show a surprising reluctance to join us. Maybe they think we'll ruin their economy, and maybe they're right.

The characteristic of New Zealanders that we find funniest is their language, particularly their vowel sounds. To our ear, they are saying that they eat fush and chups, and when they seek accommodation, they go flet hunting.

It came as a shock to Australians in 1994 when it was revealed that soon we would all be talking like that. Janet Holmes, Professor of Linguistics (or should we say lungustucs?) at Victoria University, said the English language is undergoing a vowel shift. She said New Zealanders had already moved to pronouncing these words the same: 'ear' and 'air', 'here' and 'hair', and 'beer' and 'bear', and Australians were on the way. Et least ut wull make communucation easier.

96
flies

*t*here's a puzzling omission from the journals of the 18th century Europeans who explored the coastlines of Australia—a creature that is now so common that the gesture of brushing it away is called 'the great Australian salute'. Not even those two meticulous observers, James Cook and Joseph Banks, made any mention of encountering it in the course of their wanderings around the east coast in 1770. And yet, by the end of the 19th century, flies were part of the national identity. Did the whites bring them to Australia? No, but they brought cows and sheep.

Flies like to breed in moist dung and, in a land where they had only dried-up kangaroo and emu droppings to choose from, they had a low survival rate. When the cows and the sheep imported from

Fly Romance

Of all the dung heaps in all the pastures in all the world, she flies into mine...

Europe and South Africa started leaving their precious gifts all over the landscape, the flies started a breeding festival which got bigger every year. Now that Australia has 137 million sheep and 24 million cattle, the flies are bound to be our constant companions.

The biggest nuisances are the bushfly and the sheep blowfly, both of which kill farm animals by spreading disease. CSIRO scientists have begun a program of spreading a breed of super dung beetle across the countryside to break up the flies' breeding medium. Long term, they think, we'll be spending a lot less energy on the great Australian salute.

97
our pets

*W*e don't know the name of the first dogs that arrived in Australia—that event happened some 7000 years ago when the people arriving from Indonesia with dingos had no way of recording it. But we do know the name of this continent's first cats—Miss Puss and Tom Puss, who travelled with the Rev. Richard Johnson in the First Fleet, arriving in January 1788. In naming his pets, Johnson started a great tradition of originality. The Petcare Information and Advisory Service announced in 1995 that the five most popular cat names in Australia are Cat, Puss/Pussy, Smokey, Tiger and Sooty. The five most popular dog names are Jessie, Dog, Max, Ben and Sheba.

There are 2.9 million cats and 3.8 million dogs distributed among 4.1 million Australian house-holds. Of the 66 per cent of Australian households that have pets, 42 per cent care for one or more dogs, 31 per cent have one or more cats, 22 per cent have birds and 16 per cent have fish. About one in three dog owners also has a cat.

The pattern of our pet ownership has not changed over 10 years. This distinguishes us from America, where dogs are declining while cats are on the rise. Their explanation is that the traditional nuclear household is disappearing as both parents go to work, or marriages break up, or people prefer to live alone. So Americans are moving to easy-maintenance cats. It would seem that Australia still has the time and the space to be a doggy nation.

A survey by the CIBA insecticide company in 1995 showed that 75 per cent of Australia's dog and cat owners let their animals into the house and often into their beds. And 75 per cent of dog and cat owners say their pets have fleas. So Australians have many more household pets than they bargained for.

98
our key dates

☆ **JANUARY 1**: the New Year's Day public holiday, sometimes proposed to be called Federation Day to honour the amalgamation of six colonies into one nation in 1901.

☆ **JANUARY**: the schools are closed and so are most offices, as Australians go to the beach or stay home watching cricket and tennis on TV. The Sydney Festival tries to entice people to cultural pursuits such as plays, concerts and exhibitions.

☆ **JANUARY 26**: the Australia Day public holiday, commemorating the establishment of the Sydney convict settlement in 1788.

☆ **FEBRUARY**: the school year begins.

☆ **FEBRUARY 14**: Valentine's Day, an American card-sending ritual increasingly popular in Australia.

☆ **MID FEBRUARY**: the Perth Festival of the Arts.

☆ **FEBRUARY/MARCH**: the Gay and Lesbian Mardi Gras parades through the streets of Sydney, attracting homosexuals and curious heterosexuals from all over the world. Sydney now rivals San Francisco as the international gay capital.

☆ **MARCH 7**: a public holiday called Labour Day in Western Australia and Eight Hour Day in Tasmania. They are both celebrating the same thing—the time in 1856 when members of the Stonemasons' Society in Sydney became the first workers in the world to have their ten-hour working day reduced to eight hours (though they still had to work six days a week). Labour Day is celebrated in Victoria on March 8, Queensland on May 3, and NSW and South Australia on October 4.

☆ **MARCH 8**: International Women's Day, when businesswomen affirm their inroads into traditional male domains.

☆ **MARCH**: the Adelaide Festival of the Arts happens every even-numbered year. It was the first of Australia's gatherings of theatre, literature, music and painting, and is still regarded as the most avant-garde. Melbourne celebrates its Moomba festival with a street parade.

☆ **LAST SUNDAY IN MARCH**: daylight saving ends in most states, so clocks go back one hour and darkness seems to come very early, signalling the beginning of winter and the football season.

☆ **MARCH/APRIL**: public holidays for Good Friday and Easter Monday. Fewer than 50 per cent of Australians go to church. The traditional custom of giving chocolate rabbits as gifts to children is gradually being replaced by giving chocolate bilbies (an endangered native rodent).

☆ **APRIL 1**: April Fools' Day, when harmless hoaxes are encouraged, but only until midday. Be sceptical of anything the media say on this day.

☆ **APRIL 25**: public holiday for Anzac Day.

☆ **SECOND SUNDAY IN MAY**: Mother's Day, on which Australians visit their mothers, and give them presents, especially chrysanthemums.

☆ **JUNE 14**: a public holiday in all states except Western Australia, supposedly to celebrate the Queen's birthday. Western Australia holds its Queen's birthday holiday on September 26. The actual birth date of Queen Elizabeth is April 21, but nobody celebrates that day, not even the British. June 14 was actually the birthday of King George V, who died in 1936, and this holiday used to be called Empire Day, honouring our links with Britain. As ties with Britain grow less fashionable, there are moves to change this holiday's name again.

☆ **FIRST SUNDAY IN SEPTEMBER**: Father's Day.

☆ **MID OCTOBER**: the Melbourne Arts Festival.

☆ **LAST SUNDAY IN OCTOBER**: daylight saving begins in most states, as clocks go forward an hour, signalling the start of summer and the cricket season.

☆ **FIRST TUESDAY IN NOVEMBER:** Melbourne Cup day.

☆ **NOVEMBER 11:** Remembrance Day, when Australians are supposed to observe two minutes' silence in honour of the dead of World War One. Many Australians remember it as the day in 1975 when the Prime Minister, Gough Whitlam, was dismissed by the Governor-General, John Kerr, because the Opposition parties in parliament were refusing to pass Whitlam's budget.

☆ **THIRD WEEK OF DECEMBER:** summer school holidays begin.

☆ **DECEMBER 25 (OR NEAREST WEEKDAY):** public holiday for Christmas.

☆ **DECEMBER 26 (OR NEAREST WEEKDAY):** public holiday for Boxing Day. The annual Sydney to Hobart yacht race begins, covering 630 nautical miles and attracting up to 170 starters.

99
achievements

*P*assing over such details as an 8.5 per cent unemployment rate and 1.9 million people classified as below the poverty line, Australians have a lot to be proud of. We're a cheerfully multicultural society without extremist violence. We have a national health system, funded by a tax levy, which gives everyone access to free treatment from hospitals and general practioners. Any woman can obtain a safe abortion if two doctors believe giving birth would endanger her physical or mental health. We have outlawed discrimination on the basis of race, gender, age or sexual orientation. And our standard of living puts us at number 19 position among nearly 200 nations.

Here's a sampling of some other things Australians might boast about ...

☆ **THE WORLD'S LARGEST OYSTER,** *Ostrea hyotis*, which can weigh up to 3 kilograms, is found along the Barrier Reef (the world's longest coral reef).

☆ **THE WORLD'S FIRST CALL GIRLS** were operating in Melbourne in 1891, when brothel owners set up a system of ordering by phone.

☆ **SOUTH AUSTRALIA** was the second place in the world, after New Zealand, to give women the right to vote—in 1894. And it was the first place to allow women to stand for parliament.

☆ **THE WORLD'S FIRST FEATURE LENGTH FILM** was *The Story of the Kelly Gang*, made in 1906. It used the actual armour worn by Ned Kelly and was so sympathetic to the gang that the Chief Secretary of Victoria banned it from being shown around Kelly's territory in case it encouraged public disorder. The world's first movie review, in the *Bulletin* magazine of 24 January 1907, said: 'These splendid bushrangers never came within a hundred yards of a woman without taking off their hats.'

☆ **THE WORLD'S LARGEST ANT**, the bulldog ant, which can grow to 4 centimetres, is found in northern Australia.

☆ **THE WORLD'S FIRST GOVERNMENT ADVISER ON WOMEN'S ISSUES** was appointed by Prime Minister Gough Whitlam in 1973. She was an Adelaide solicitor named Elizabeth Reid.

☆ **THE FIRST FLIGHT ACROSS THE PACIFIC** was made by an Australian, Charles Kingsford Smith, from Oakland, California to Brisbane, Queensland, in 1928. In the same year,

Kingsford Smith also did the first flight from
Australia to New Zealand, and the first
nonstop flight from Sydney to Perth.

☆ **THE WORLD'S LONGEST CONTINUOUS
FENCE**, 1.8 metres high, runs for 5531 kilometres through central Queensland and NSW,
designed to keep dingos away from sheep.

☆ **THE WORLD'S FIRST PENSION FOR
WIDOWS** was introduced by the NSW
government in 1926.

☆ **THE WORLD'S HEAVIEST CRAB**, *Pseudo-
carcinus gigas*, which can weigh up to 14 kilograms, is found in Bass Strait, near Tasmania.

☆ **AUSTRALIA** produces 95 per cent of the
world's opals, and the world's biggest, the
Desert Flame, weighing 6800 grams, was found
at Andamooka, South Australia in 1970.

☆ **THE WORLD'S BIGGEST PEAR**, a monster
weighing 1.58 kilograms, was grown at
Turnbull's orchard, Ardmona, Victoria, in 1987.

☆ **THE WORLD'S FIRST JUVENILE COURT**
was set up in 1890 in Adelaide, designed to
protect young defendants from public scrutiny
and 'any criminal taint'. (The USA set up its
first juvenile court in 1899.)

☆ **THE WORLD'S FIRST PARLIAMENTARY
ELECTION BY SECRET BALLOT** was held
for the Legislative Council of Victoria on 27
August, 1856. Britain didn't introduce secret
ballots till 1872 and the American state of

Massachusetts introduced them in 1888.

☆ **THE WORLD'S FIRST WOMAN DETECTIVE THRILLER WRITER** was Mrs Fortune, who published *The Detective's Album: Recollections of an Australian Police Officer*, under the pseudonym 'W. W.' in Melbourne in 1871.

☆ **THE WORLD'S FIRST NOTEPADS** were the Silvercity Writing Tablets that went on sale in Launceston, Tasmania in 1902. The idea of gumming sheets of paper together along the top came from a stationer named J. A. Birchall.

☆ **THE EAGLE WITH THE BIGGEST WING SPAN** in the world (up to 3.5 metres) is Australia's wedge-tailed eagle.

☆ **THE WORLD'S FIRST ROUND-THE-WORLD PASSENGER SERVICE** was started by the world's longest-surviving airline, Qantas, in 1958 (Sydney to London via USA in five days).

☆ **THE WORLD'S FIRST PREFERENTIAL VOTING SYSTEM**, whereby voters could number candidates in order of preference, was introduced in Queensland in 1892.

☆ **THE FIRST SHOT FROM THE ALLIED SIDE** in World War One, and the first shot from the Allied side in World War Two, were both fired by Australians—in fact both from Fort Nepean, near Melbourne. On 4 August 1914, the fort fired on a German ship attempting to leave Port Phillip Bay, and on

3 September 1939, the fort fired on an unknown ship approaching Port Phillip Bay.

☆ **THE WORLD'S FIRST TROUSERS WITH PERMANENT CREASES** were produced in 1957 by the CSIRO. The process was patented as 'Si-ro-set'.

☆ **THE WORLD'S LONGEST EARTHWORM**, *Megascolides australis*, which grows up to four metres, is found in Gippsland, Victoria.

☆ **THE WORLD'S FIRST COMPULSORY VOTING** was introduced in the Queensland elections of 1915, when Labor won for the first time.

☆ **THE WORLD'S FIRST 'BLACK BOX'** flight recorder was designed by David Warren of the Aeronautical Research Laboratories, Melbourne in 1958.

☆ **THE LONG LIFE PLASTIC BAG**, which keeps vegetables fresh for six weeks by filtering out ethylene, was invented by two Melbourne chemical engineers in 1993.

☆ **THE OLDEST MARATHON WINNER** was Cliff Young, a Victorian potato farmer who ran from Sydney to Melbourne in five days 15 hours in 1983, aged 63.

100
our symbol

*t*he bronzed outback hero probably never existed. If he did, he's dead now, of drought, bushfire or skin cancer.

index

INDEX

INDEX